Adjusting the Sails

Adjusting the Sails

Weathering the Storms of Administrative Leadership

Donya Ball

ROWMAN & LITTLEFIELD
Lanham • Boulder • New York • London

Published by Rowman & Littlefield
An imprint of The Rowman & Littlefield Publishing Group, Inc.
4501 Forbes Boulevard, Suite 200, Lanham, Maryland 20706
www.rowman.com

86-90 Paul Street, London EC2A 4NE, United Kingdom

British Library Cataloguing in Publication Information Available

Library of Congress Cataloging-in-Publication Data Available

ISBN 978-1-4758-6702-2 (cloth : alk. paper) | ISBN 978-1-4758-6703-9 (pbk. : alk. paper) | 978-1-4758-6704-6 (ebook)

♾™ The paper used in this publication meets the minimum requirements of American National Standard for Information Sciences—Permanence of Paper for Printed Library Materials, ANSI/NISO Z39.48-1992.

For my children,
Benjamin, Allyson, Jacob, and Sephina.
May you adjust your sails with the changing tides.

For my husband, Rilian,
The voyage as your first mate is just getting started.

For my parents, Teymour and Robin,
The true definition of persistence and resilience through the storms.

For my brother, Dax,
The one who first taught me how to lead without
fear no matter how big the waves.

Contents

Preface ix

Introduction xi

Chapter 1: Haters Gonna Hate: Adjusting to Your Unpopular Position 1

Chapter 2: Circus: Juggling the Demands of Life and Leadership 13

Chapter 3: What Are You Talking About?: Effectively
Communicating in Top Leadership 21

Chapter 4: Own It: Developing the Courage to Admit Your Mistakes 37

Chapter 5: The U Word: Surviving and Thriving during Union
Negotiations 47

Chapter 6: Passed Up: Rebounding after Career Disappointment 57

Chapter 7: The Pandemic Pivot: Learning Flexibility and Strength
in the Face of Disaster 67

Chapter 8: Progress Is Progress: Keeping Your Focus on the Right
Goals 75

Chapter 9: Branding: Public Perception Is Everything 91

Chapter 10: The Journey: Remembering the End Goal 103

Bibliography 113

About the Author 117

Preface

Before we begin, find your favorite reading spot and pour yourself a glass of your favorite beverage.

"You can't make this stuff up." These words are often whispered in principals' offices and muttered in superintendent meetings around the world.

But isn't it the truth? You couldn't make this stuff up if you tried. The insane experiences, constant disappointments, and immediate changes that administrators face can send the best leader into a tailspin.

There is no road map that helps top-level administrators navigate successfully through the cruel and often scary world of administrative leadership. There are no exact recipes for career success, no go-to manuals, and no quick fixes.

Sure, there is an abundance of literature that reminds us of important leadership behaviors. But what about the war stories that really shape us? No one really talks about the real-life experiences that educators wade through day after day.

It is a common occurrence to sit in silence at the end of each day reflecting on a baffling question: "What just happened?" Luckily for me, I have surrounded myself with several high-quality mentors who lighten the burden. Through tears, angry outbursts, and laughter, they share their war stories with me.

We all need that camaraderie: the power of shared stories. Otherwise, loneliness and hopelessness will creep into the empty spaces between the questions.

My experiences, both personal and professional, have shaped who I am as a leader. As I have walked through the journey of educational leadership, it has been the crazy heartaches, the celebrations, the student successes, and the staff setbacks that have impacted me in a profound way.

There is power is in the lessons embedded in each of our unique stories. It is not the peer-reviewed research, the dry manuals, or the massive amounts of studies that have resulted in good leadership. Instead, the real power lies in down-to-earth leaders who have the ability to self-reflect, internalize the lesson learned, and apply them to the future. We each have stories, war scars, and experiences that need to be passed on to a new generation of leaders.

These are the stories that we need to share. They will give us courage, equip us for the days ahead, and provide the strength we need to go where no one has yet gone: into the future. Most of all, they will teach us how to adjust our sails in response to changing circumstances.

What does it really take to be a successful educational leader? The secret to success is being *a leader that continuously inspires others to do the right work on behalf of students.* But the practical outworking of these principles is what you rarely get except through nitty-gritty daily experience.

As I lived these day-to-days stories, I constantly muttered to myself, "This will be in my book someday." Today, I present this book to you. It is a reflection drawn from intimate, personal reflections on my daily struggles and triumphs. As I imagine you going through the same situations, I impart dozens of practical tools that you can apply to your unique situation.

This book also focuses on the unique challenges facing female administrators. It is no secret that although 76% of teachers are women, less than a quarter of our nation's superintendents are women. Why is that? Although the rate of women entering site and central office leadership positions is increasing, it can be a cruel world out there if we are not resilient to the big challenges. Women need to be equipped with the skills and strengths we need to succeed. Most of all, women need the heart-to-heart conversations from fellow administrators to assure, "I've been there. It's hard. I see you, and I believe in you. You can do this."

My hope is that you will find comfort and peace knowing you are not alone. When you face downright insane experiences, they will make you want to throw in the towel. During those difficult times, I hope this book encourages you to go on. Stay the course. Cry. Mourn. And pick yourself up because your students need you. They need strong, courageous educational leaders who can overcome adversity and roadblocks.

Administrative leadership is an unsteady ship that can make even the most skilled sailor quite nauseous. You will experience rough seas. But do not go overboard. You can weather the storm by adjusting the sails. Let's raise our glasses to that.

> "The pessimist complains about the wind; the optimist expects it to change; the realist adjusts the sails."—William Arthur Ward

Introduction

Soon after entering the world of administrative leadership it became apparent that life was about to get a whole lot more interesting. Although my teaching career was full of its own challenges, the administration felt like I was the starring role in a reality television show. Before the career advancement, I recalled my mentors often advising, "Just remember, it's lonely at the top" but nothing could really prepare me for the rough seas of administration until I took the plunge.

Although all of us administrators have juicy, shocking stories, we do not often talk about the struggle. On the surface, we suck it up, put our best foot forward, and attempt to survive each storm. But secretly, we often wish that there was a book we could escape into—a book that was truly aligned to our reality. Now, this book that is in your hands.

The challenging experiences, humiliating disappointments, and mind-boggling changes of leaders can confound the best of leaders. I show you how to face these challenges with grace and poise. Each chapter is a storm that you must learn to survive if the goal is to have a long, successful career as site or district leader.

Having served in administration for several years, I not only bring a wealth of experience and empathy to administrators of every stripe, but I also have spent years listening and observing what successful leaders do. And even more importantly what ineffective leaders do.

Whether you are just beginning your journey or well along the path of leadership, you will learn to admit mistakes, develop communication skills, pivot during disaster and crisis situations, and build a branding strategy to present yourself effectively to the watching world.

The text begins by focusing on the jarring changes and adjustments that brand new administrators face. First, administrators will need to adjust to the loss of popularity and public acclaim. You will learn to deal with haters and respond well to criticism. The second chapter focuses on another surprising change: the increased demands of leadership. Administrators will learn to juggle seemingly endless responsibilities with grace and humility. These essential first lesson of leadership will help new administrators acclimate to their new role in top leadership.

We then transition to the skills that develop during middle leadership: communication skills, owning mistakes, and effective negotiation. Effective communication skills can make or break a leader, so we will look at strategies for impactful one-on-one conversations and memorable meetings. In addition, good leadership communication includes the ability to admit your own foibles and flaws. Finally, we will look at practical skills you can use throughout the big union negotiation process.

We will then discuss the skills a maturing leader acquires at the site or district level. These chapters focus on keeping your eyes on the goal through career disappointment, community and global disasters, and everyday difficulties all while maintaining a confident, positive public image and presenting yourself to the world.

We wrap up by revisiting the purpose and rewards that give meaning to our jobs in top leadership. What makes administration worth it? What motivation will keep you moving on the toughest of days? This is what you will discover in the final chapter.

Each chapter outlines principles of leadership, grounded both on research and personal experience to weather each storm. These strategic approaches to navigate even the wildest of tides I call The True North: the concept of administrative leadership processes that works as a compass to guide you from the current conditions to calm waters.

This book will serve as your navigation as you embark into a difficult leadership world for which there is often no reliable guide. Relatable anecdotes and practical guidance will help you weather the storms and adjust your sails to navigate the ever-changing tides of the educational world.

Chapter 1

Haters Gonna Hate

Adjusting to Your Unpopular Position

Attention People Pleasers. Take a deep breath and pour yourself a big glass of wine (or drink of your choice). You're about to hear some very unpopular news.

Get ready: Being an administrator is a hard, unpopular job. Your days of being universally and extravagantly adored are over.

"But I was a great teacher," you may say. "Everyone loved me."

Yes. As a teacher, you were the center of attention. Students brought you chocolate roses on Valentine's Day. Kids drew messy crayon pictures of you standing with them under a rainbow and flowers. It wasn't uncommon to hear, "You're the best teacher I ever had!"

Parents loved you, as well. Some were more vocal than others, but you could tell they all genuinely appreciated you. During the coronavirus pandemic, parents came to your doorstep begging for your help. "How do you do it every day?" they asked, frazzled from the effort of keeping their first grader on task all day long.

And your principal really loved you. She appreciated you as the over-achieving, workaholic professional that not only had well-behaved students but *high-performing* learners. She was grateful that you allowed her to go about her daily duties without causing her any worry or concern.

But administration is different.

The select few teacher leaders who become administrators believe they will continue to truly be loved by everyone. After all, what is there not to like about your new position? You will support teachers, listen to parents' complaints, and just keep the system running smoothly.

But the bad news is that when you become an administrator, you step out of your popularity position. You enter a world of being disliked, judged, and criticized. Statistically, high-level leaders are distrusted 19% more than immediate supervisors, simply because of their position.[1] Unfortunately, now that you have reached top leadership, you will no longer be able to please everyone.

Well, that is only partly true. It *is* possible to please people and be an administrator. People-pleasing administrators will make it through, but at a huge cost. They will sacrifice their success. There is no way to truly succeed as an administrator and also please the people in your care.

You see, administration requires *cajones*. It demands brave soldiers who aren't afraid to charge forward in the direction they believe is right, even at the expense of popular opinion. Real leaders need bravery. They need to be ready for the battle. And they need to very quickly learn to be okay with being disliked.

This lesson will hit home quickly after the honeymoon period of your first administrative job. Most likely, you start out an assistant principal. You eagerly embrace your new position: serving the top administrator, who appears to be loved and adored by all the staff.

Although everything looks rosy at first, you aren't prepared for what's ahead. You quickly discover the gaps and deficiencies in the school. You clearly see the problems in the supposedly fail-proof approaches and habits of your well-loved principal.

Now, you find yourself in a most challenging situation. You want to address the weak points of the school. However, you know that causing waves and disrupting the beautiful harmony of the school is definitely not on your priority list.

Being stuck in this tough spot is common, but it's not easy. Thankfully, you're relieved of this burden by another promotion not too far off in the distant future. As an assistant principal who is on great terms with the district, you are promoted to your first principalship. You are excited and full of pride. You believe you're equipped to do an amazing job.

Being a principal is every new administrator's idea of a Dream Job. If you are a current principal, you may chuckle at the thought of being in a dream job. But the truth is that most assistant principals do not retire as assistant principals. They each look forward to being the captain of the ship.

The first few months of the principalship are filled with invigorating experiences. Staff treat you to your favorite coffee. Students greet you eagerly at the gate each morning—the highlight of your day. You begin testing your long-term leadership capabilities, enjoying the freedom of working towards change without having to bow to a higher authority in the building.

And then, like a blow out of nowhere, you are also confronted with your first major crisis. Like a house fire that wakes you up during the night with blaring alarms, the smoke of emergency blindsides and blinds you. The reality of being a principal hits you like a sudden blow out of left field. BAM!

When you arrive at school one morning, Chandra is waiting to see you. She is one of your beautiful, hippie, tree-hugging teachers, and you wonder why she looks so concerned. Cautiously, you open your office door and ask her to have a seat.

In a nonchalant, calm voice, Chandra proceeds to tell you that a few parents will be calling the school to complain. Why? Well, it's a long story. The day prior, when a parent volunteer was in the classroom reading a story to Chandra's students, that parent distributed small, plastic baby fetuses to the class. The parent then proceeded to share that these babies are a gift from God and need to be protected. The fetuses were taken home by the kids, as they were a present from the parent.

Chandra felt too bad to intercept the babies. She just wants you to be aware of a potential issue. As she leaves the office, she gives you one of those plastic fetuses. It's a souvenir for your first fire.

Alone in your office once again, you sit in shock. You spend a few minutes feeling sorry for yourself. But soon, you realize you need to charge through the smoke and take decisive action to put out this fire before it grows. As a leader, it is time to gear up for battle.

You'll need to address two issues: the teacher and the parent. But practically, how do you do this? Credential programs do not train you for these very real experiences, let alone teach you how to deal with pro-life propaganda given to students. Sure, it is common to look for advice and direction from the district office, but the fact of the matter is that no one is going to have time to delve into these personal conversations with you. In a very real way, you are on your own.

Feeling like a fish out of water, you lose sleep as you rehearse over and over the conversations that will follow. At the same time, you wonder if you will show up to your school and see a banner proclaiming, "Welcome to Administration." The sign would indicate that this was all a sick joke. You almost hope it was.

Through guidance from the district office, you realize that you will need to give the teacher a written memorandum of understanding. After all, she allowed the parent to go off script into an area not approved by the curriculum. The parent will also be informed that she can no longer volunteer in the classroom for the remainder of the school year, since she was not granted permission to share this content with the students.

The advice sounds great, and you eagerly follow through. But as soon as you've delivered this unpopular news, the reality of your new position begins to truly sink in. Both the parent and the teacher are furious. The reality slowly turns your insides cold. You are no longer the popular teacher receiving roses on Teacher Appreciation Day. Instead, you're the unpopular leader who is "causing all the problems."

The teacher may choose to gather the troops. Her family and even fellow staff members will back her up as she challenges your decision. In addition, the parent may fight back. Angry parents are notorious for throwing around the "attorney" word. They often even follow through with threatening lawsuits. These situations can scare the crap out of a new principal.

The peaceful, tree-hugging teacher and the fetus-loving parent can easily become an even bigger issue. This situation has the very real potential of becoming a Union problem. Chandra and the site Union rep, and potentially even the district Union rep will meet with the principal for the sole purpose of removing the memo of understanding. The principal decides to refuse this compromise, as consequences exist for even adult misbehavior.

The powerful reps will use intimidation towards you as a young principal. They think you are easily swayed. Trying to stay true to what you believe is right, you feel bewildered. You sit there in disbelief, wondering why in the world you once thought this would be a Dream Job.

Sound familiar? These conversations of conflict are not typically short, are they? In fact, they usually last hours and result in pure exhaustion. Every person explains their desires over and over again. Realizing there that the teacher has clearly made a misstep, the Union will usually end up backing down a tad. But the absolutely critical move is that you as a principal do not back down.

You may feel tempted to give in to their requests and become a People Pleaser all over again. But at what expense? You would sacrifice the success of the organization. You absolutely cannot have both. You cannot be liked, and at the same time do the right thing for your school or district.

People are waiting for you to fall, and they will not catch you on the way down. As a principal, you become a human punching bag. However, once the battle is over, you will know that you have gained the respect from the Haters. In fact, it is your adversaries who will be talking about you over the dinner table with their own families. They will share about how well you composed yourself and stayed true to the cause.

Staying calm in the face of hatred and opposition is not easy. These situations absolutely cause stress. But they also provide a valuable lesson. You will learn very early on that people will not be happy with you as a leader. In fact, they will be downright angry. How fortunate are the administrators that have such a profound event happen early in their administrative careers.

What are some practical tools you can use to meet these situations with poise and determination? How can you learn to avoid the worst of the battle, while staying true to your convictions? What can you glean from those who have gone before? Here are some tools you can have at your disposal as you charge into the flames.

BE PATIENT WITH THE PROCESS

The whole idea of being unliked as a leader does not come naturally to many. Sure, you have been told the importance of facing problems head on. But by the time you made it into administration, you've likely spent years pleasing others.

It took a lot of work and education to become a school administrator. Wasn't pleasing others the goal of much of your early schooling and career? During that time, you strove for affirmation from college faculty and even your own family to support your professional career aspirations. You tried to please professors, bosses, and administrators above you.

Now that you're a principal or superintendent, the mindset shift can be unsettling. Being vehemently disliked can come as a shock to the system. Having people upset with you is very uncomfortable for you as a leader, just as it is for everyone else. This important lesson takes time to learn. Be patient with yourself as you digest the implications of being in top leadership.

Remember that having thick skin gets easier with time. Try to keep the big picture in mind. Remember that you're learning a new skill that's unfamiliar to you. As you encounter more and more situations, you'll adjust to your new role and the lack of popularity it entails.

At the beginning, you lose a lot of sleep over being the bad guy. You're in a world that feels like a tornado. The first few years, you have a lot of sleepless nights, thinking about the people who are upset with you. However, with time, it gets much easier.

Why does it get easier? It's not because you get accustomed to being mean. Quite the opposite. You start realizing that "being the bad guy" is just another term for standing up for what is right. Doing the right thing absolutely benefits kids, staff, and families.

When you stand by your convictions and core values at a time when you are really pressured to go outside of them, it always ends up serving you well. When you see how the district or school benefits holistically from your stand and approach, you gain the courage to keep on keeping on. As you go through that cycle over and over and over, you start seeing the rewards of that process. Even though people have been pissed at you, you continue to do what you need to do.

The patterns of consistency and leadership that you are building will take time to develop. When you're doing it for the first time, you haven't experienced the reward. But when you stick with the process and give yourself time to adjust to the demands of leadership, you will find that it gets easier with time.

PARTNER WITH THE HATERS

Even though conflict is inevitable in administrative positions, there are practical steps you can take to minimize the harm. Success as a leader requires the ability to take on the challenging employees, the devil's advocates, and even the people who you believe are not "in it for the kids." Your job is not just to take them on, but to partner with them.

Say what? Partner with them?

How do you partner with challenging people who hate you? What are realistic ways to do that? First, you need to clarify what it *doesn't mean* to partner with those who dislike you. It doesn't necessarily mean the two of you develop a friendship. You don't have to form a social relationship outside of work.

What it does mean is that you create opportunities, whether during the workday or outside the workday, to really listen to this person with intent. Here is a practical approach you can use with someone who absolutely has it out for you: invite them to coffee. Or to a Zoom call. Say, "Hey, I want to learn more about your perspective on this topic."

During that meeting, do a lot of listening. Allow the other person to do a lot of talking. Your goal is not necessarily agreement. Instead, the goal is for the hater to see that the leader is truly vested in understanding the other perspective.

Furthermore, your goal is to receive useful information that you can use to humbly modify your approach on the issue. Let the person know that you will take their views into consideration. You may not do a total 180- or 360-degree turn based on what they share. It probably won't change your mindset altogether, but it may give you a new idea or perspective. Let the person know that you are open to change.

For instance, imagine there's a staff member that really dislikes their principal or another teacher. You are the superintendent, and this person comes fuming into your district office, deeply upset.

"Didn't you get my emails?" they accuse. "You're not listening to my concerns. I've reached out repeatedly, and you're not doing anything about this problem principal."

It would be easy to write this teacher off. You could dismiss their concerns by saying, "You're just a complainer. You're always high maintenance with these types of issues. You just need to accept it."

In fact, you may really like the principal they're complaining about. You may feel tempted to become adversarial with the teacher. After all, they are experiencing extreme anger that seems out of proportion with the problem.

Understanding that "haters gonna hate" will help you take this situation in stride. Instead of dismissing or defending, you can embrace the other person's thought process. You can listen with intent. You can try to truly gauge an understanding of the root of the issue.

For example, the teacher may be complaining, "The principal is never around. We don't know what he does. He's always in his office. He's not in classrooms. We don't even feel like we have a principal." Listen to this concern, then see if you can find the problem that underlies the principal's absenteeism.

Sure, it's a valid concern that he's not visible in his building. But perhaps the root issue is that he's putting out fires in the office that the staff member isn't even aware of. Perhaps he's disciplining kids, dealing with angry parents, or doing other invisible tasks.

Your job as a leader is to get to the root of the issue. Go back to the principal and ask him what is really going on. Say, "Hey, staff perception says that you're absent from this campus, that you're just collecting a paycheck and sitting in your office eating donuts. What is it that is going on? Help me understand."

If the principal is being bombarded by something extreme, you will need to support him with that issue. As you help mitigate that problem, you are addressing the root problem. You are helping to fix the problem the staff member is complaining about.

None of this would have ever been possible if you had taken the staff member's attacks personally. If you had tried to please the staff member by saying, "Yes, yes, I'll fire the principal," you would have handicapped the process of growth.

When you realize that "Haters are gonna hate," you learn to accept these challenges. You can listen to the haters, deal helpfully with their concerns, and partner with the complainers. At the same time, you can work for change in a way that doesn't short-circuit your problem-solving process.

Work together with those who seem to hate you. View them as teammates who help you get to the root of issues and problems in your organization. As you partner together, do not give up hope that even the biggest adversaries can in fact become the biggest advocates and cheerleaders.

Eventually, you will get to the point where you realize that surrounding yourself with people who challenge you is critical. The key to organizational growth is the ability to constantly improve. How will you do that by staying in the safe zone of people who constantly comply and agree? That is not an option. Embrace the ones who do not like you. Soon, you might become friends. You might find yourself treating them for dinner or their favorite booze.

Don't assume that every hater will become a permanent enemy. Look for things you may have in common. Try to get them on your team. Whenever possible, take the first step to get on the other person's team. You're the leader. You can take this powerful step to bring peace.

MITIGATE HARM FROM HATERS

It's important to get "thick skin," learning to be ok with being disliked. But there are also many strategies you can use to try to prevent, deal with, and diffuse hateful comments when they arise. You can mitigate the harm of opposition, disagreement, and conflict. You can smooth out the haters' thoughts before they even begin. Here are some other tactics you can use to not only survive, but also mitigate and prevent, the inevitable criticism.

Hold Parent Forums

Parent Forums and District Listening Sessions can be a powerful way to minimize the harm from haters. For example, a brand-new superintendent in the Midwest hosted 20 listening sessions as she prepared to craft a new vision statement for the district. She reports, "During the listening sessions, participants were asked what the district did well, what are the challenges and how the district can change culture through communication."[2]

When you hold a similar listening session, you will give students, parents, and community members a chance to voice their opinions. They will be less likely to act hateful and oppositional when they are being given an explicit opportunity to share their feelings.

During the forum, practice your listening skills. Let your community members feel that their voice is making a difference. Give an opportunity for the haters to state their point of view. Respond openly to the challenges so that the whole school and district community see you as a problem solver.

As you develop thick skin, don't become callous to others' needs. Open your heart to the real-life conflicts and concerns that your community members have. Take their concerns into consideration. That way, when the die-hard haters express their opinions, the rest of your community will back you up. They know that you are willing to listen and solve problems whenever possible.

BE A FORWARD THINKER

Prepare for the protests. Anticipate the anger. Count on the controversies. In other words, think ahead to what areas of concern might be coming down the pipe, and prepare your response in advance.

When you're dealing with parent and community concerns, you as a leader need to be forward-thinking. You need to know how to respond ahead of time to what the potential problem areas may be. Take an offensive approach of prevention rather than a defensive stance of reaction.

If a parent, Union member, or community forum catches you off guard, you are in a precarious spot. You'll feel the hatred more personally and be tempted to make unwise decisions. If someone brings up an issue, law, or piece of legislation that you have no idea about, you'll be left standing there like a deer in the headlights. You'll think, "Oh no! How do I answer this?"

On the other hand, if you've done your homework as a leader, you'll be able to anticipate what the concerns or outrage are going to center around. You'll read up on legislation and local and state politics that can result in community revolt. You'll rehearse in advance how you will respond. "If a parent asks this, I'll say this." You'll head into the meeting or forum or discussion with more confidence.

Use your forward-thinking to anticipate the objections or concerns the naysayers may bring to the surface. To the degree possible, deal with these issues before they become a big deal. Reassure your community that you've seen these problems coming and have already stepped in to deal with them. This will give them a deep sense of reassurance.

Here's a boots-on-the-ground example. After the pandemic, some districts instituted a COVID vaccine mandate for school-aged children. In order to attend public school, children were required to take the vaccine. As a principal in one of these states, it would be relatively easy to see that this issue will cause a lot of controversy. Due to all the upheaval and conflict that has already surrounded COVID-19, it is easy to anticipate that there will be conflict around this decision.

This is where you as the principal or superintendent need to step in with your forward-thinking hater-prevention karate moves. You must anticipate that some parents will be totally supportive of this concept, but you must also expect that other families will be diametrically opposed to the mandate. Even though they may be fine with the laundry list of vaccines their children have already received, this particular vaccine will feel too new to them.

Take action. Step in. Do your research. Understand the viewpoint of the government of the state that has issued the vaccine mandate. Work to comprehend the state's reasoning. Why did they think the mandate was necessary? What specific details or concerns led up to creating this new law?

In addition, take the time to read up on all the nitty-gritty practical details. Find out the timeline. Is the mandate going to take a phased-in approach? Will all grades be vaccinated at one time, or only certain grades? Your research will help you answer families' questions intelligently.

As you do this investigation ahead of time, you prepare for whatever may come. With your forward-thinking, you can anticipate the questions that the community, staff, or parents are going to ask. In fact, you can send out messages that inform and reassure parents before they even start their hate speech. You can stay a step ahead of what people are going to say. In this way, your listeners will form a strong perception that you are not only knowledgeable about the issue, but confident in responding to the demand.

Another area where you can practice forward-thinking is in the area of gifted education. Parents care a lot about their children's success, and it's important to them to know that their gifted kids are being sufficiently challenged in the classroom. They'll often come to you with an ultimatum: "I think my kid is gifted education material. What are you doing to ensure that my student is being challenged?"

You as a leader need to be prepared to answer this very common question. Have your pulse on the school's or the district's policies on gifted education. Know the curriculum and strategies that are in place for students to continue to be challenged.

This way, when a parent questions you, you'll be able to say something intelligent. You won't be tempted to fall back on a vague reassurance: "Oh, they're being challenged, I'm sure of it." You'll be able to articulate the different ways the teachers are helping the student reach his or her full potential.

Each school district carries its own load of unique problems and situations. As a superintendent or principal, it's up to you to spot these issues ahead of time. As you read the news and deal with daily situations in your school or district, always scan the environment for potential issues. Consider the problems that might mushroom into something big. As you gain experience, you'll get faster at recognizing these potential threats. Try to head off the haters before their influence becomes all-pervasive.

THE TRUE NORTH

School and district administration requires thick skin, but it's more than that. Being the "bad guy" requires skill and expertise. To deal with the haters, you must:

- Stand strong in the face of challenging, hateful opposition.
- Do what you believe is right.
- Give people a chance to share their opinions in a safe place so that problems do not escalate.
- Be aware of situations that might turn into bigger problems down the road.

There are always going to be Haters. Haters Gonna Hate. But what is your response going to be? Your students are depending on you to stay calm, to see things from multiple perspectives, and to listen to your haters. The haters' valid points will keep you growing. As time goes on, you'll chuckle at this ironic part of leadership. These are the stories you can't make up: the ways you grew, even in the midst of the hate.

NOTES

1. Charles Feltman, *The Thin Book of Trust: An Essential Primer for Building Trust at Work* (Bend, OR: Thin Book Publishing, 2021), in "Highlights of The Thin Book of Trust: An Essential Primer for Building Trust at Work," https://www.tacoma.uw.edu/sites/default/files/2020-09/thinbookoftrust.pdf.

2. "Superintendent Dr. Alicia Thompson shares feedback from listening sessions," Wichita Public Schools, accessed November 17, 2021, https://www.usd259.org/site/default.aspx?PageType=3&DomainID=2766&ModuleInstanceID=13639&ViewID=6446EE88-D30C-497E-9316-3F8874B3E108&RenderLoc=0&FlexDataID=22054&PageID=8977.

Chapter 2

Circus

Juggling the Demands of Life and Leadership

Driven, determined, confident. These words describe many administrators. Along the way to the top, you've juggled dozens of responsibilities. You've performed almost superhuman feats to keep your life, your children's lives, and your school duties afloat.

You proved to yourself and those around you that you were more than the challenges life threw at you. Somehow, you're still kicking. But it hasn't been an easy road. Some days, you feel like a crazy circus clown, juggling more balls than you can handle.

Perhaps you started your career like many young teachers do. Although you enjoyed the classroom, your original dream was to be a stay-at-home mom. You loved teaching, but you were willing to put your career on hold to welcome a tiny human into the world.

You'd always admired those "model moms" you saw on Instagram. That ultimate stay-at-home mom was the pinnacle of productivity. As you scrolled through social media, you vicariously watched her sip her daily dose of Cafe Vienna, then spend her day carpooling, grocery shopping, laundry, ironing, and making dinner. She maneuvered through household duties with class and grace.

After giving birth to your first child, you were bound and determined to be just like that supermom. You'd take the stay-at-home route. You'd succeed with flying colors.

But after a few days on your new job, you found yourself collapsing on the couch with only one thing to say: "This job is hard!" Many days you looked forward to hanging out with the neighborhood mom across the street over a glass of Chardonnay, just to have a little bit of a breather from 24–7 mommy duty. You suddenly gained a new level of respect for all stay-at-home moms everywhere. How did those moms on Instagram do it, anyway?

Suddenly, teaching began to feel like a viable option again. When you started considering going back to teaching, you wondered if you were selfish. All the women in your church small group seemed to imply that you were. Whispering behind your back, they looked at you in shock as they mouthed, "How could you?" Some even said it out loud: "Do you really have to?" "Why would you choose that?"

Your mom guilt may have made the whispers seem more extreme than they really were. But at the same time, it felt like there was no compassion. You realized that women can be extremely cruel and judgmental to one another.

Despite the judgment, you knew deep down that sometimes a lady just needed to work to be truly fulfilled. You knew you were not the only one who thought this way. Finally, you decided to take the plunge back into teaching. You found it filled a need and scratched an itch like nothing else.

Welcome to the circus.

When you plunged into teaching after your first child was born, you realized that teaching was more complicated now than it was before kids. There were many additional facets to your new life. Being a full-time mom was not easy, but neither was juggling your children's needs *and* your teaching role at the same time.

But you were strong, capable, and determined. You needed to keep showing yourself and the world that you could handle the demands of full-time work and full-time mothering.

Kids kept coming one after another, and you kept climbing the administrative ladder. Once you were "all in" with teaching, the jump to administration was a short one. With a master's degree behind you, you found yourself eyeing a place in administration. Why not go even farther doing what you loved most: organizing and monitoring systems of improvement? Your superintendent saw your strengths and offered you your first administrative position. You felt like you were walking on air.

Now, you're facing the acrobatic act of working and administrating while juggling full-time mothering. As you keep track of one child in grade school, one in a different preschool, and one on the way, you begin to fear for your job, your role, and your future. You seek to prove yourself in the administrative arena, and you wonder how your children will reflect on your future prospects. No matter how high your confidence in your own abilities, you fear that others will not see you the same way. A pregnancy, a sick child, or too many responsibilities at the same time may threaten your prospects. As you adjust for needs at home, you fear that others will begin to see you as incompetent.

To push back against that perception, you work as hard as you possibly can. Nine months pregnant, you're still trundling through the halls, putting out fires in your school. Perhaps you're even in the classroom, conducting a formal observation, when the labor pains hit.

After the baby is born, you are bound and determined to continue breast-feeding. Wanting the best for your children, you hide in the closet or bath-room to pump for your little ones. Or you take a walkie talkie to the nearby day care at lunch and nurse your baby on the couch just to make sure you do not miss out on any pressing issues back at school. Every day is a constant balancing act.

The circus doesn't end there. Once in administration, you feel the need to get more education. A doctorate degree feels like the perfect way to fulfill a personal goal and hone your professional skills. Deep into school adminis-tration, you see areas where you need to grow and develop. Going back to college seems perfect for your needs.

Again, people ask, "Why now?" "Your kids need you." "You're taking on too much." But you know that more important than anything else is the driv-ing force that has been behind all your juggling over the years.

What is the driving force? It's the determination not to lose yourself in the midst of all the chaos. You want to keep using your gifts. You don't want to disappear beneath a pile of humdrum chores.

You know you can take it all on, so you press on. When you set a goal, you can make it a reality. So you push forward.

Juggling all these areas, however, comes at a cost. You suddenly discover that there are things you simply can't hold together. You find yourself drop-ping balls. This leads to one of the most important lessons you need to learn as you juggle the administrative life: have grace for your failures.

GRACE FOR FAILURES

As you try to keep track of all the aspects of your new life, it's easy to let some things slip. One of the easiest areas to drop is your marriage. Administrators are constantly growing and learning, but they often forget to bring their partners along for the ride. As you evolve and grow professionally, you often forget to grow closer to your partner.

Your spouse may be incredibly supportive of your career and educational aspirations. But he or she may still resent the sacrifices that come along with your professional goals. Long working hours, board meetings, constant fires to extinguish, and multiple out-of-town conferences can make a marriage unsustainable over the long haul if you let it.

Without knowing it, you may be overburdening your relationship with your loving partner. When you disappear into the next room to write your dissertation, zeroed in on your career goals, you forget that you've left your spouse alone to make dinner and tend to the family. Without realizing it, you're forcing the one you love the most to sustain these sacrifices year after year.

Perhaps you assume your relationship is more durable than it really is. At the back of your mind, you know that it's not easy for your spouse to be married to such a driven professional. But you assume that your partner can handle the short-term sacrifices while keeping the end goal in mind. You long for your spouse to be your solid friend, understanding the reasons you choose your career and higher education.

It's easy to succumb to the idea that ending the marriage will ease the situation. You might want to find someone who truly understands this new you—or choose to be alone—in the dark abyss you believe this will be better than your current reality. You feel bad that you don't try harder to "make it work," but you find yourself bailing on your marriage.

Before you know it, you've dropped some major balls. You will need to take some steps to recover your circus act before it's too late. One of the most important things to remember is that there is always forgiveness available.

Recovering from a major misstep like divorce, failure, or mismanagement can require intense therapy and forgiveness. Picking up the balls you've dropped takes courage, humility, and determination. Learning to coparent, learning to accept your failure, and learning to start juggling again is a difficult but beautiful process.

As you handle the circus of life, remember that there is always grace. You can receive restoration, forgiveness, and new beginnings. There is always time to start over, no matter what mistakes you've made. Each time you make a fresh start, you do so with a little more wisdom and balance and a few more tools under your belt. Life is full and continues to be a chaotic, beautiful mess. Remember that even a master juggler drops many balls, but he always picks them up and starts again.

SET BOUNDARIES

As you juggle your professional and personal responsibilities, you should ask yourself an important question. "Is this my only option? Do I have to spend the rest of my life chaotically grabbing at responsibilities as they fly towards me? Are all these responsibilities really as important as they seem?"

If you're asking these questions, you're headed in the right direction. You don't always have to live like a crazy circus juggler. There are important ways that you can choose to let go of some of the balls you are juggling. Prioritize the most important responsibilities and delegate the rest to others.

Although leaders must learn to balance personal and professional life well, they must also master the art of saying NO. Just because you wear many hats doesn't mean you have to wear every hat that people try to assign to you. You as the leader are the one who chooses which responsibilities to take on and which to let go of.

Suppose a teacher texts you on a Friday night. She's in a frenzy, worried about a student and parent situation. It's an emergency, she says. She's hoping you'll be willing to meet with her over the weekend. She's sure you'll want to help her out. She ends her text by reassuring you that she's so grateful for your support.

As you set down your phone, you sigh. You're feeling a mix of resentment, resignation, and confusion. Should you really give up your chill Saturday afternoon to help this teacher out? It seems like she's desperate. You remember how grateful you've been in the past when one of your mentors sacrificed their time to meet with you on their day off.

You pick up your phone to tell her you'll meet with her.

But then you pause. In your mind's eye, you see your kids begging you to take them to the park. You remember that you'd promised them you'd take them this weekend. In addition, you know that if you don't take a break, your own mental health will suffer. You won't be the leader you need to be without taking proper time for rest and recuperation.

Your resolve strengthens. Just because this teacher feels it is an emergency doesn't necessarily mean it really is one. Her situation can wait. You don't need to panic, even if the teacher does. You can work with her to find a time that works for both of you early next week.

You remember the mantra: "A lack of planning on your part does not constitute an emergency on my part." You realize that you don't need to overwhelm your calendar just to rescue people from their own mistakes and emergencies. Instead, you can give people space to work out their own problems. You can show them that you trust them to figure it out on their own.

Filled with determination, you text the teacher back. "I can't meet tomorrow, but I can spend a few minutes texting with you about your emergency tomorrow afternoon. Then we'll work together to find a time that will work for you next week."

Learning to set boundaries is an important part of maintaining your sanity. You must take the time to rest, recharge, recuperate, and relax. It's important to maintain your own mental health by saying "no" to some of the balls people throw in your direction. Sometimes, it's ok to take off some of the hats and let your hair down.

PRIORITIZE MENTAL HEALTH

Prioritizing your staff's mental health is another way to cut down on the responsibilities piling onto your plate. Think about it: a relaxed, healthy, calm teacher is less likely to dump her issues and concerns onto you. Help your teachers build peer support systems. Encourage them to lend a listening ear to one another. This way, they will not try to make you responsible for fixing their breakdowns.

This doesn't mean that you must take on the burden of starting another program for your teachers. You don't need to create another initiative or babysit your staff's mental health, all by yourself. Instead, you can ask the staff themselves what they need in order to decrease stress. Put teachers at the helm, allowing them to take charge of their mental health. Assure them that you'll provide the needed resources to help them along the way.

For example, perhaps the teachers, counselors, and classified staff could start a Positive School Culture Committee that meets once a month to share ideas. Staff can handle this role on their own without any intervention from you. They can meet periodically to discuss the stress levels of teachers in the buildings. They can support each other, debrief, and brainstorm about steps that can be taken to raise positivity in the culture.

You'll be surprised at what your staff can come up with all on their own. They might make a mental health wellness bingo card full of simple wellness activities: listening to music, trying a new hobby, smiling at a student, or reading a book for fun. They might fill a basket with low-budget snacks teachers can receive as prizes for completing their bingo card. They might compete with each other as they track their mental health-boosting wellness activities. The smiles, laughter, and fun that are added to the building will bring joy to your heart. Their simple ideas can be cost-effective and easy to implement.

When you as a leader intentionally support positive staff wellness, it will also help you manage your own stress level. As you help your staff maintain a positive work-life balance, it will reduce the emergencies that are offloaded onto you.

As a side note, allow your staff to take a break when needed. There are plenty of time-clock Gestapos out there who will enforce bell-to-bell work schedules. Do not be one of those annoying leaders. Those that you supervise will thank you tremendously for your trust and respect of their mental health.

Staff anxiety causes urgent "fires" that they want you to solve. They try to rope you into putting out the fire. But mental health programs help staff put out stray sparks before they grow into emergencies. When you help staff manage their own mental health, there will be less urgent situations piled onto your plate. Make sure staff are aware of the insurance options or district wellness opportunities that will help take advantage of professional counseling or therapy.

As you're prioritizing your staff's mental health, don't forget about your own. Do you need to take a vacation? See a therapist? Take some time for self-care? Do whatever is necessary to keep yourself in a good mental space. Allow others to help you carry the weight of your daily responsibilities.

Don't try to do it all alone. Recognize that vulnerability with trusted friends and coaches is an important—and needed—self-care practice. If you are struggling with the weight of the responsibilities you're juggling, make sure to ask for help sooner rather than later.

REMEMBER THE END GOAL

Education administration is more than a work-home balancing act. It is a circus. It is conducting a performance. It's a well-choreographed production. And it takes multiple takes and even sometimes a whole new design of the script to make it work.

As you continue to work and rework your plan, keep in mind the end goal. Is it worth it? Absolutely, but only if you're able to truly give yourself grace during the times of crazy.

Be patient with yourself during the seasons when you feel that you are doing nothing well. When your kids are sick, and you have to meet with the angry parent anyway. When you have to choose between the board meeting and the swim meet. And neither choice seems like the right one.

Why is it worth it? It may take more than a decade to find out. But when your first born is a focused high school student excelling in athletics, your middle child has her mind set on accomplishing a 100-mile endurance horse ride, and your youngest son is a happy go lucky jokester, you'll begin to feel a sense of gratitude and satisfaction. You tell yourself that somehow, all of this hard work on momma's part has influenced them all in some way. Of course, in the silence of reflection, you wonder. You wonder if you could have done it any better.

THE TRUE NORTH

Life can be a circus. It is a roller coaster ride, full of ups, downs, and in-betweens. But through the disasters and heartache, there are also celebrations. There are times of rebirthing happiness, drenched in complete thankfulness for the experiences that have shaped you.

Along the way, remember these key ingredients to surviving the circus:

- Give yourself grace for the times you drop the balls
- Focus on mental health
- Remember that the journey is worth it, even if you don't see it right now.

The work is hard. Balancing administration, parenting, and marriage is extremely difficult. But know it can be done if you truly work through the chaos. Seek affirmation in knowing that not only are you changing the world, but your children are watching as well. There can be a lot learned from administrative jugglers. And when one of your children drops the ball in their own life, they'll immediately know the outcome . . . pick it up and try again.

You got this.

Chapter 3

What Are You Talking About?

*Effectively Communicating
in Top Leadership*

When you first step into administration, you feel very confident in your technical skills. You know you are good at evaluating curriculum, crunching numbers, and planning budgets. You're excited about monitoring learning and organizing systems of improvement.

But before the first month of administration is over, another reality hits hard. If you want to be truly successful as a top-level leader, you will have to master the challenge of effective people skills. In administration, it's all about communication.

Communicating as a principal requires mad skill. First, you need to learn to communicate with stressed parents, students, and teachers. Dealing with the hot-tempered parent, the difficult student, and the upset teacher are not for the faint of heart. Quickly, you realize you have to gain a whole lot of soft skills that you weren't taught in school. Curriculum choices and perfect spreadsheets will mean nothing if you can't calm the flustered person in your office.

You quickly enter the School of Communication. Here, you learn by trial error throughout the pain of daily life. You learn to master the art forming your next statement while the person is still talking. You find out how to read people's facial expressions and emotions. You'll learn to be quick on your feet, to be direct and at the same time nonoffensive.

In the School of Communication, you'll meet some very interesting characters. When you hear their stories, you'll learn to approach all people with compassion and listen before you speak or jump to conclusions. You'll learn not to judge too quickly. Day in and day out, you absorb lessons of kindness and honesty.

When conversations get heated and your heart beats a little faster, you'll learn how to navigate your way through tough emotions and situations. You'll learn to reason with people, bringing relevant arguments and information to bear on the situation. You'll learn the importance of being swift and yet not rushed. You'll learn to end the conversation with respect, even when there is not agreement. And most important, you'll learn that words truly do matter.

In her book, *Fierce Conversations,* Susan Scott says,

> Our work, our relationships, and our lives succeed or fail one conversation at a time. While no single conversation is guaranteed to transform a company, a relationship, or a life, any single conversation can. Speak and listen as if this is the most important conversation you will ever have with this person. It could be. Participate as if it matters. It does.[1]

The conversations you have with others, whether in small groups, one-on-one, or in a boardroom, are critically important to your success as a leader. Let's look at some key skills that will help you level up in the School of Communication.

COMMUNICATING ONE-ON-ONE

The first area where you will need to grow is in your ability to relate one-on-one. Whether you're meeting with a parent, staff member, or student, you'll need to be able to communicate care and concern while remaining true to your goals and leadership values. Paying attention to these skills will help you save time and waste less breath. Learn these lessons on the front end instead of waiting to learn them the hard way.

Be Vulnerable

As a strong leader determined to retain your poise in front of haters, you probably cringed as your read the word, "vulnerability." When you think of vulnerability, you often think of dumping classified information about your foibles and failures on other people.

The good news is that being vulnerable doesn't necessarily mean that you have to divulge your deepest secrets in front of parents. You don't have to cry at a meeting or spill your weakness to the staff member who is complaining in your office. In fact, Brené Brown clarifies that oversharing is the opposite of true vulnerability. She says, "Vulnerability is based on mutuality and requires boundaries and trust. It's not oversharing, it's not purging, it's not indiscriminate disclosure, and it's not celebrity-style social media information dumps."[2]

Instead, vulnerability simply means making the choice to show up to situations that are uncertain. It's the courage to engage, even though you know you can't control the outcome. Brené Brown explains, "Vulnerability is . . . engaging. It's being all in."[3]

Brown believes that the rigors of leadership will automatically leave you feeling exposed and uncertain—or vulnerable. That's not a choice. Your choice is whether or not you will choose to continue to show up to the harrowing task of leadership, day after day.

She explains,

> Vulnerability is not weakness, and the uncertainty, risk, and emotional exposure we face every day are not optional. Our only choice is a question of engagement. Our willingness to own and engage with our vulnerability determines the depth of our courage and the clarity of our purpose; the level to which we protect ourselves from being vulnerable is a measure of our fear and disconnection.[4]

All conversations include uncertainty and risk. As a result, it's common for new administrators to try to avoid engaging with others. You hem and haw before important conversations, trying to find a way out. If you think of enough excuses, you can justify ignoring the problem.

Questions run through your mind:

"How do I tell him x, y, and z?"
"How do I open up the conversation?"
"Should I even have the conversation?"
"Can I escape this?"

It's natural to feel nervous. Being fearful of the conversation is okay. But avoiding the necessary conversation because of your fear is not acceptable. Neglecting important conversations will ultimately start a small flame than can spread to a full-on fire. The entire department will have to get involved with extinguishing it! Being vulnerable includes embracing the uncertainty of walking into the flames.

Will you continue to show up to conversations? When you have no idea what the other person is going to say or what concerns they are going to present, are you willing to go to the meeting anyway? Will you reach out rather than hide in the shadows?

Journey Together Towards the End Road

During a tough conversation, you often know the goal of your verbal exchange before it even starts. Usually, your goal is not to have a friendly conversation. Instead, you usually need to deliver some type of bad news that the other person doesn't want to hear.

As a result, it's tempting to dump your message on your hearer and walk away. It's easier this way. You can get it over with more quickly. Instead, it's important to you that your conversation is a journey. You need to bring your listener along with you towards the end destination.

Move towards your goal slowly and intentionally. Go at a pace that your hearer can understand. Practice the art and craft of conversation. Allow your conversation partner to walk with you towards the end road.

Although you already know the outcome you're hoping for before the conversation takes place, remember that your listener often does not. It's important to help the other party understand why the meeting is heading towards a certain unpleasant outcome. In addition, allow the other person to have a say in how the conversation goes.

Suppose you want to have conversation with an employee about their performance. Your first-year fifth-grade teacher's lack of classroom management has become noticeable, and it's high time to talk to her about it. As a principal, you're pretty convinced that she is not suited for this position. It's time to address some much-needed situations that have gone under the radar for far too long. So you call a meeting with her to express your concern.

When she arrives at the meeting, she's already anxious. She's wondering, "What's the principal going to talk to me about? Am I going to be fired? Am I going to be written up?" With these thoughts running through your teacher's head, how should you start the conversation? Should you lead with brusque words: "You are not fit for this job. Goodbye"?

As you can imagine, bluntness is a terrible strategy. It's better to lead her gently towards the end road. Perhaps she will make this conclusion on her own. She will see for herself that she would be more successful in a different career.

Start by asking the teacher how she believes the year is going so far. Let her talk. Allow her to see that you are truly listening. Perhaps she will come right out and say she is struggling. Or maybe she will say everything is going perfect.

Either way, you listen. If she does not segue to classroom management, then you gently guide the direction of the conversation. You say, "Let's talk about student engagement. Do you think your students are highly engaged most of the time?"

As she struggles for words, she will probably begin to talk about her stress levels. She'll mention how horrible things have been lately, how parents are on her tail, how difficult the students are this year, and how she's just miserable.

In the process, you want to listen for the exact words she uses. Using her own words to move the conversation is a powerful tool. As you guide her in the direction of discussing her performance, utilize phrases and concepts she's already used in conversation.

For example, if she's talking about stress levels, you can say, "The stress sounds really difficult this year. I wish I could help you through this. I want to support you. I'm sensing how upset and stressed you are. What can I do to help you be more successful?"

As she stops and reflects, she may list some things you can help her with. Or perhaps she'll look at you helplessly and say, "I don't know." Either way, you have given her an opportunity to ponder and self-assess.

If she's miserable and can't think of any ways that you can support her, you're very close to your end road. You can easily say, "I'm wondering if you would be happier in another career and position." You've reached the same conclusion you set out to reach: letting her go. But you've done it in a gentler way.

This conversation is so much more productive than it would have been if you'd said right off the bat, "You're done." You've given the employee the opportunity to talk to you. You've given her the understanding of why this has happened. You've allowed her own voice to tell the story, rather than telling it to her yourself.

Perhaps your employee says, "I need your help with this, this, and this." You can then provide support via instructional coaching or various resources. You should come to the meeting prepared to offer specific and detailed resources and coaching.

After offering her support, you can still arrive at the same end road. You're just getting there by a different route. You can say, "If I support you in all these ways and you still find yourself in a world of stress, perhaps this isn't a career that brings you deep satisfaction. If I support you and there's still evidence that you're not able to meet these expectations, then we're going to really have to have a conversation about whether this career is the right one for you."

You've reached your end road by a different path. You heard the teacher begging for help. You've offered her support. But as a forward-thinking principal, you aren't automatically optimistic. You have mentioned the possibility that even with help, the teacher will not be capable of fulfilling her responsibility. You've outlined the consequences if her performance does not improve, even with assistance.

Though this teacher may not leave the conversation feeling like a rock star teacher, she will nonetheless leave the conversation with the feeling that she had the opportunity to state her stance. She knows she had the chance to share how the year was going from her point of view. As for you, you've gained a powerful new perspective that will help you proceed as you evaluate her response to the specific and tailored resources.

Thinking in terms of the end road requires you to be ready to move forward your intended response, no matter what the other person is saying. As they're talking, you are already framing your next piece of conversation. Anticipating the journey of conversation takes a lot of practice and is difficult to do. But it's necessary to guide the conversation to a productive place where there's resolution.

Finding the end road allows you to steer the conversation towards the place you want it to go, without creating unnecessary anger and anxiety. If you just state the desired outcome at the beginning, you set yourself up for stress and pain. Don't just get to the meeting and blurt out, "You're done." This would be tragic to the employee. And it doesn't help them understand how to improve. Instead, guide the interchange towards the ideal outcome that you have in mind. Steer the other person to make the conclusion themselves, so you don't have to say it yourself.

Whether you're talking to a parent, teacher, or student, know the goal you hope to accomplish in the conversation. But first, allow the individual to state their view of the situation. Really take time to listen, then guide the conversation back to your initial objective, this time considering the things the person has shared.

This leads to one of the most important ingredients in communication: listening.

Learn to Listen

No matter what communication role you are playing, listening plays a vital role. Listening is a powerful tool, even more important than the actual talking that you do. Listening gives you the chance to form your power talk. Learn to stop, reflect, and ask yourself, "Am I really listening?"

Truly learning to listen takes practice. Imagine this familiar scenario. A parent, teacher, or colleague has asked for a meeting to discuss their concerns. You've set a time for the meeting, but you're still not at ease. You know this is not going to be an easy conversation.

The participants arrive, and the meeting begins. With a big sigh, the perturbed party starts stating their concern. You grimace as you listen to their accusations.

Nonetheless, this is the critical part. It's your turn to play a crucial role. It's time for you to listen.

Do not interrupt. Do not get emotional. Stay calm and firm. Allow others to see the love and compassion you have for your job.

It's difficult to see the big picture during the high stress conversation, and it's hard to stay focused on a good outcome for the exchange. It's tough to listen to what the other truly is saying, while at the same time attempting to form to your next dialogue. This fine art takes time to learn. It does not come naturally to most, and it takes practice.

Give Your Full Attention

As you practice your listening skills, you may be tempted to take detailed notes of everything the other person is saying. You may feel compelled to get a record of the hateful and unfair things the other person is stating about you. Or you may want to write down your own thoughts so you don't forget your comebacks.

Taking notes during a conversation can seem like a great idea. It provides wise documentation on your part, and it helps divert the intensity of eye contact and direct listening. However, please recognize that note-taking can also have the reverse effect. It can imply to your conversation partner that you're not really listening and don't deeply care about the interaction.

When you take notes constantly, you send the message that you do not trust your own leadership instincts and human ability to facilitate conversation. Instead, you imply that you need to be able to refer to every single little thing that took place, most of which is not even worth referencing again.

There is a difference between jotting down bullets or short phrases and writing an entire novel of *everything* that is being said. It's okay to write down key takeaways and to-do items. But make sure to maintain a balance. Seek to demonstrate your confidence in yourself and the attention you are giving to your conversation partner.

Be Honest

Simon Sinek said, "It is better to disappoint people with the truth than to appease them with a lie." While it's often tempting to hide the facts, leadership requires honesty and transparency with those you serve. Susan Scott continues on the same theme: "Everyone wants one person in the world to whom they can tell the truth and from whom they will hear the truth. Become that person."[5]

Susan Scott says that leaders often hide the truth in conversations. She's not saying they necessarily lie; they just don't tell "the whole truth and nothing but the truth." Scott suggests asking yourself these questions to help you clarify the level of truth-telling that is going on in your organization:

- How often do I find myself—just to be polite—saying things I don't mean?
- How many meetings have I sat in where I knew the real issues were not being discussed?

- What has been the economical, emotional, and intellectual cost to the company of not identifying and tackling the real issues?
- When was the last time I said what I really thought and felt?
- What are the leaders in my organization pretending not to know?
- What am I pretending not to know?
- How certain am I that my team members are deeply committed to the same vision?
- What is the conversation I've been unable to have with senior executives, with my colleagues, with my direct reports, with my customers, with my life partner, and most important, with myself, with my own aspirations, that, if I were able to have, might make the difference, might change everything?[6]

Susan Scott says that leaders often show up to conversations carrying their weapons. Their statistics, tasks, commands, and directives serve as shields that protect them from the real content of the honest conversation. Often, leaders don't actually seek to connect on an emotional level with the individuals on their team. Nor do they vulnerably reveal the emotional investment that they as leaders feel. In a way, this lack of authenticity is a form of deception.

Susan Scott emphasizes that you need to be honest about the emotional content involved in the situation, both for you and for the other parties involved. No one wants to be "talked to. We'd rather be talked with," Scott explains.[7]

Rather than lecturing your teachers from a detached and cold perspective, make sure to approach them kindly and listen wholeheartedly to what they say. Make sure you are honest and authentic about what you are really feeling.

Don't hide behind your position as a leader. Come out from behind your metaphorical shields and present the true emotional stakes you have in a situation. Reveal your truth and allow others to reveal theirs.

Be Willing to Learn and Grow

As you read these conversation tips, you may feel a wave of fear and apprehension. You've likely had several of these tough conversations—maybe even this week. You wish you could avoid them altogether! But unfortunately, that's impossible in the world of administration.

You will not only have the conversations, and you will often make mistakes. Tough conversations require you to be humble, recognize your own failure, and admit, "I really screwed up that one." All in all, they are a chance to learn and grow.

After the conversation, you will have a chance to sit back, replay the exchange in your mind, and think about you could have done better. Each tough conversation is a practicum in the School of Communication. It's a way to put into practice the tools you're learning. After each self-evaluation, you will realize that you are growing incrementally in the School of Communication.

The art of conversation is difficult to learn from a manual. It takes everyday experience and the willingness to learn and grow. At the same time, it's also important to do some book learning. Surround yourself with mentors and authors who can help you learn communication skills. Read books and go to classes to improve your conversation skills.

As we've already discussed, *Fierce Conversations* by Susan Scott is a wonderful book for a new administrator's professional reading list. Another excellent resource is *How to Have That Difficult Conversation* by Henry Cloud and John Townsend. This book helps you get to the heart of what happened and acknowledge the role each person played in the problem. It helps you understand the riskiness of talking about emotion, the fear involved when someone's worthiness and love seems to be at stake in the conversation, and how to let go of things that are truly not important.[8]

Reading books and going to conferences will shore up your confidence and give you tools that you can use in the everyday, on-the-ground experiences of life. It's the practice and experience that will make you more confident in hard conversations. Your first one will be difficult, but they will get easier as time goes on.

It's easy to fall into unhelpful patterns sometimes, which is why it's important to reflect and improve over time. Keep a growth mindset, realizing that you will make mistakes! Keep yourself enrolled in the School of Communication, and you will continue growing towards your goal of effective leadership.

RESPECTFUL GROUP COMMUNICATION

Those one-on-one personal conversations are tough. When tensions are up and people are yelling in your face, you gain a new perspective on the difficulties of leadership communication.

But it's equally tough to communicate with groups. It's not exactly simple to speak to disengaged teachers who are exhausted at the end of the day, wishing they didn't have to attend another staff meeting. Words matter when dealing with parents and students, but they also matter when administrators communicate with the teachers in their care.

John Maxwell said, "Communicators take something complicated and make it simple," but "educators take something simple and make it complicated." Unfortunately, this quote is not too far from reality. How can you learn to communicate your vision and dream in group settings, without boring your teachers and staff to tears?

Allow for Teacher-Driven Problem Solving

When teaching kids, everyone understands the importance of allowing students to lead the way in their own education. Science has shown that children become more motivated when they're involved in their learning. As a result, schools are shifting away from teacher-driven talking to a student-driven classroom in which students take a major role in determining their learning outcomes. Even though there are widely varying opinions on the ever-controversial Common Core, both fans and naysayers can agree on one thing: When students talk and initiate discussions, powerful learning happens.

Why can't staff meetings follow the same wisdom? Rather than lecturing, why couldn't administration give more power to the teachers in the conversation? When facilitating meetings, try giving the conversation over to the teachers and subordinates, allowing them to truly be the problem solvers. Allow for discussion, utilize focus groups, and initiate panels. Let your teachers provide each other with peer support and listening. Let them solve their own issues in the way that works best to them, and watch the magic happen.

Leader Rounding

If you've ever spent time in the hospital, you've likely awakened multiple times during the night as the nurses do their nightly rounds. They check on their patients, assess their needs, and assure that they are doing well.

In a similar way, the concept of Leader Rounding involves checking on your staff members and ensuring they are doing okay. This is an element of care and communication that you can incorporate into leadership meetings. Be assured, staff will start looking forward to meetings when they realize that their leader will genuinely take an interest in their needs and feelings.

The concept of rounding is a very important way to give power back to teachers. Ensure that you incorporate this powerful tool into your next meeting. Take the time to check in on your teachers and ensure they have what they need.

As an administrator, your "rounding" will extend beyond making literal rounds of the school building. Although it's important to walk around the school during the day and check in with classes, you'll never be able to get the whole story during the school day. Instead, it's important to structure your leadership meetings in a way that ensures you hear from each teacher and validate their unique needs and concerns.

In a nutshell, here are the basics of rounding. The facilitator of the meeting asks each person a series of questions to set the stage.

1. What is working well?
2. Do you have what you need to do your job?
3. Is there anything I can do to help you continue to perform well?
4. Is there anyone that has been especially helpful to you?[9]

Rounding can be used in a variety of ways. You could try starting every monthly management meeting with these questions. Or you could incorporate them into your regular interaction with your department chairs. How about going on a retreat with the grade-level leaders? In short, rounding can be used successfully in medium-sized groups, as well as in one-on-one meetings.

One-on-one meetings can give you the chance to ask these questions personally and really listen to the answer. Find out how the year is going and listen to their thoughts about planning for the future. As the principal, you might schedule rounding appointments with your staff periodically throughout the school year. As a superintendent, you may meet with principals from time to time to ask these questions.

As you utilize rounding, you will not only find out what the current challenges are, but will also discover what the current needs are. This simple activity brings out all sorts of information you would not have known about otherwise. It allows you to begin to address stressors before they mushroom into giant emergencies. You'll uncover areas of support and ways you can jump in. You'll use this information to make the year run as smoothly as possible for the hard-working teachers or principals in your care.

After you've put your finger on the pulse of your staff through rounding, it's important to take their concerns seriously. Take time to summarize the common themes that are coming up frequently in your teachers' complaints. Ensure that you prioritize the concerns that are most pressing and decisive.[10] Afterwards, check in with your staff members to see whether they feel their concern has been adequately addressed.

After just a few months of demonstrating this type of tangible support and care, you will notice a variety of responses. Perhaps you'll see teachers crying from stress, grateful to have a listening ear. Or perhaps they'll be laughing with joyful happiness. Having an outlet for their emotions will be meaningful to your staff. When you give them a voice and shift the power from you to them, you'll see your teachers blossom before your eyes.

Respect Teachers' Time

Have you ever noticed how much educators talk? A 30-minute IEP meeting stretches to two hours, just because educators love to hear themselves repeating the same thing over and over again. Leadership meetings only have time to cover the first two items on the agenda before the one-hour time allotment expires. Bored and exhausted educators constantly check their phones and watch the clock, displaying their anxiety to get the heck out of the room.

Meanwhile, frustrated superintendents threaten their staff: "If you don't stay focused, I'm going to make you leave your phones on the central table."

How does this help? Such a ridiculous and disrespectful idea doesn't even get close to addressing the root cause of the issue. If the content being presented by the administrator were engaging and necessary, teachers would tune in of their own volition.

Administrators need to emphasize the same time usage principles that they constantly harp about with classroom teachers. Principals constantly evaluate teachers' effective use of instructional time, often referred to as bell-to-bell instruction. They emphasize high student engagement. When it comes to the classroom, everyone knows the importance of wise use of time.

But administrators are not running the same show at the top. Deep down, they know they are having meetings just to have meetings. Teachers complain about admin wasting their time—and many administrators would agree with them.

Having a clearly scheduled end time helps you respect the time constraints of your teachers. Then, make sure you wrap up the meeting at the agreed-upon time. If you didn't get through all your material, schedule a follow-up conversation to respect the time of all parties involved.

Furthermore, take the teachers seriously when they say they need more time. Instead of adding another meeting to announce the next brand-new initiative you've added to the laundry list, try surprising them with an unexpected break. Teachers love it when you say, "I recognize that we are all overwhelmed. I know that you need time for x y and z. There will be no meeting today." Try this genius move and watch the positive feedback you receive!

Define Your Intentions

What's another way you can address these long-winded meetings with very few outcomes? You can clearly define the intentions that you have for your meeting. Find the nugget of truth you want to present, then speak about it briefly and succinctly. Try to eliminate everything that is not absolutely necessary.

Ask yourself: "What is the essence of what I need to communicate? What am I really talking about? Are the agenda items so absolutely critical that I will be able to keep my colleagues' attention? Or could 99% of the topics be covered in an email memo?" Being more purposeful in your dialogue is one way you can respect your staff's time and ensure that the work is accomplished in a reasonable time frame.

Perhaps you are unsure what the purpose of your upcoming professional development session is. In that case, why have it? You say you are supposed to have x number of staff meetings or PLCs a month, and you feel you need to stick to that. Really? They are called Purposeful Conversations for a reason. If you do not know why you are having them, then you have a major problem.

In her book, *Fierce Conversations,* Susan Scott provides some thought-provoking questions to help you define your intentions. She says, "Ask yourself . . .

- What are my goals when I converse with people?
- What kinds of things do I usually discuss?
- Are there other topics that would be more important given what's actually going on?"[11]

Do not barge into meetings unprepared. Don't make speeches on the fly. Most importantly, don't confront important issues and sensitive subjects half-heartedly, flying by the seat of your pants. Here are a few ways to make sure you are ready for an important meeting.

- List out the most important points of the conversation prior to the meeting to ensure you stay on topic. What are the key takeaways you want your listeners to get from your meeting? How can you ensure you don't ramble on and on about random topics? Most of all, how do you want your audience to feel when you are done? Are you aware of the "emotional wake" that you will leave behind?[12] Ensure that the words you choose will create the impact you are aiming for.[13]
- Meet personally with powerful, influential people before the actual meeting itself. This is what Maxwell has in mind when he talks of "the meeting before the meeting." Ensure the key players hear your point of view and have the chance to develop their confidence in your opinions. Find out the opinions of key stakeholders before you make brazen announcements.[14] Become familiar with their point of view and their likely reactions to what you have to share. In his book, *Leadership Gold,* John Maxwell goes so far as to say, "If you can't have the meeting before the meeting, don't have the meeting. If you do have the meeting before the meeting, but it doesn't go well, don't have the meeting. If you have

the meeting before the meeting and it goes as well as you hoped, then have the meeting!"[15]

- Focus on Preparation. When you're giving a presentation to a large group, it's important to be prepared. Even in personal meetings, it's a good idea to rehearse and practice. Role playing your essential statements is a great habit. Just make sure that the conversation sounds natural and doesn't come across as stilted or memorized.

Define your intentions, know your purpose, and weed out any meetings that do not move your goals forward. Whether you are facilitating a management meeting or contributing to an IEP meeting, prioritize the art of purposeful conversation. No matter what, don't approach a meeting unprepared.

Your communication skills are constantly being evaluated. Staff, students, parents, immediate supervisors, and even the board members are always watching you. When communicating with a group, be careful and choose your words intentionally.

THE TRUE NORTH

What you say and how you say it must never be ignored. Your conversation skills can make or break people's perceptions of you as a leader. If you ramble and are long winded, people will view you as scattered and unorganized. If you are hot tempered and interrupt often, people will view you as a total b*tch. Neither will score you any points as a leader.

Mastering the art of facilitating conversation is a downright nonnegotiable expectation. If you lose sleep over it, fine. If you need to rehearse the conversation ahead of time with a trusted colleague, fine. No matter what, communication is your leadership priority. Your ultimate leadership impact is on the line. The way in which you engage in conversation can make or break your retainment of employees you want in the district.

When you are tempted to give up in despair and hide from the next person who wants to talk to you, remember the importance of honing your communication skills. Your entire career hangs on this skill. Allow your goals, hopes, dreams for the future to continue driving you forward to learn and grow.

NOTES

1. Susan Scott, *Fierce Conversations: Achieving Success at Work and in Life One Conversation At A Time,* (New York City: Berkley, 2004), as quoted on Goodreads, Accessed December 2, 2021, https://www.goodreads.com/work/

quotes/16957-fierce-conversations-achieving-success-at-work-and-in-life-one-conversa.

2. Brené Brown, *Daring Greatly,* (New York City: Avery, 2015), 45.

3. Brené Brown, *Daring Greatly,* 2.

4. Ibid.

5. Susan Scott, *Fierce Conversations.*

6. Ibid.

7. Ibid.

8. Summary of "Difficult Conversations: How to Discuss What Matters Most," Accessed November 22, 2021, https://www.beyondintractability.org/bksum/ stone-difficult.

9. Casey Kuktelionis, "The Four Most Important Questions to Ask when Rounding," Last modified on January 15, 2021, Accessed November 29, 2021, https://www.studereducation.com/important-questions-ask-rounding/.

10. "QAPI Leadership Rounding Guide," Accessed November 9, 2021, https:// www.cms.gov/medicare/provider-enrollment-and-certification/qapi/downloads/ qapileadershiproundingtool.pdf.

11. Susan Scott, *Fierce Conversations.*

12. "The Six Minute Book Summary of the Book, Fierce Conversations, by Susan Scott," Last modified on August 23, 2011, Accessed November 29, 2021, http://rustedpumpkin.com/rugh-blog/ the-six-minute-book-summary-of-the-book-fierce-conversations-by-susan-scott.

13. Siddiqui, Mehreen and Alexis Lennahan. "Corner Office Chats: The Importance of Learning Public Speaking Skills." Goal Set Coach, December 17, 2020. YouTube video. 20:22 https://www.youtube.com/ watch?v=Cp7yoiMV4_s&ab_channel=GoalSetCoach.

14. Jo Miller, "The Secret to a Good Meeting: The Meeting before the Meeting," Last modified on July 23, 2018, Accessed November 29, 2021, https://www.theladders. com/career-advice/the-secret-to-a-good-meeting-the-meeting-before-the-meeting.

15. John Maxwell, *Leadership Gold: Lessons I've Learned from a Lifetime of Leading,* (New York: HarperCollins Leadership, 2008), as quoted in John Pearson, "The Meeting Before the Meeting," Accessed November 29, 2021, https://www.ecfa. org/Content/The-Meeting-Before-the-Meeting-Pearson.

Chapter 4

Own It

Developing the Courage to Admit Your Mistakes

CHEERS! CONFETTI! LET'S CELEBRATE!

When your funding is generous and you can prioritize the much-deservered raises, you pull out all the stops. When your organizational climate survey comes back with excellent results, you invite the entire staff to dinner. When your district makes progress towards its metrics, you make sure the whole building or district knows about it.

Many can relate to the exuberance of celebration. Everyone wants to promote the successes of their district or building. It's natural to rejoice when good things happen.

But sometimes, these celebrations of success are only a smoke screen for the darker side of administration. All administrators know that for every glorious success, there is a major failure. No one even thinks of celebrating their mistakes on the district's social media page. They certainly won't broadcast the bad news in a mass email to all parents and staff members.

Failure is hard to acknowledge, let alone celebrate. When have you ever heard an educational leader say, "Yes, I really screwed up with that parent today!" No one enthuses about their mistakes, goofs, and gaffes. Instead, they hide them.

Even when a leader intellectually recognizes that failures are an important learning opportunity, he or she is often more than eager to sweep them under the rug. Instead of taking ownership for failures, learning from mistakes, and moving forward with intentionality, leaders often blame others. It is common for leaders to participate in the never-ending venting and finger-pointing.

They say things that blame the parents, the community, or the environment: "That parent is crazy. There is no making him happy. What a disaster it is to deal with someone so irrational."

You too may have said all those things and more. You know you're not proud of it, and you recognize the need to take the next step of admitting what you have done. The fact of the matter is that unless leaders begin to OWN their mistakes, they will never resolve any problems. They will never have the chance to learn and grow from failure. And they will never become the solution-seekers that the organization depends on them to be.

As a leader, admitting your mistakes takes a massive amount of vulnerability. Brené Brown, an inspiring author and expert on vulnerability, explains that leaders must not only show up and put themselves in risky and uncomfortable situations. Sometimes, those risks will fail.

It's difficult enough to put yourself out there, taking risks for the benefit of the community or school. But it's another thing altogether to realize that you took a risk, failed your venture, and now need to take ownership for your mistakes. But it's a critical skill for anyone in leadership. You must be able to accept your contributions to the problems and successes of your organization.

GROWING IN HUMILITY

Taking ownership requires a mad amount of humility. You'll need to apologize when it just does not seem like you are at fault. You'll need to sometimes choose to compromise, meeting in the middle with an employee when all you want to do is let them go. Most of all, you'll need the humility to accept responsibility for the errors your subordinates have made because of your own lack of planning, communication, and leadership.

It's easy to recognize lack of humility in others. Perhaps you've seen a stark example of a leader refusing to take ownership for what was clearly their fault. In these cases, you automatically root for humility, confession, and apology.

You're the superintendent, and it's brought to your attention that a principal seems to be missing in action. She's well-loved by her staff and community parents, and she's been with the school for seven years. But lately, she's been doing a disappearing act. She's leaving most of the work of administration to the second-in-command.

This assistant principal is more versed in many aspects of leadership. In many ways, he's more skilled than the principal herself. The vice principal excels in the instructional part of curriculum, knowing exactly how to train teachers on best teaching strategies. He's also great at making human connections, creating a positive energy, and building up the school. Parents and staff love that about him.

But the staff are starting to notice that the assistant principal is basically doing the job of the top administrator. They love the way the vice principal runs the school, but they're worried that should he leave, they wouldn't have a strong leader.

Recently, the principal stood up at a staff meeting talking about her high stress level conveying her frustrations about how much is on her plate and that she is not in a good emotional space. Her intent was to build camaraderie. She wanted to communicate, "Look guys, I'm stressed. You're stressed. We're all stressed together. We can just talk about it. If you have anything on your mind, come talk to me. My office is open." She wanted to build rapport, and send out a message about how much she identified with her teachers.

Despite the principal's best intentions, this was not how the messaging came across. Instead, her staff talk conveyed a tone of uncertainty, instability, and low competence. The staff perceived that the principal didn't have what it took to lead the school during this stressful time.

Now the staff is reaching out to you, the superintendent.

"This is ridiculous. She's not able to do the job," they complain.

You schedule an appointment with the principal, hoping that she will acknowledge the way her message came across. You want her to take responsibility for what she did. If she is a true leader, she will say, "Yeah, I can see how that message is starting to change perception of my proficiency." You want the principal to own her own mistakes and work towards changing the perceptions of her leadership capacity.

But when the meeting begins, the principal does just the opposite. Instead of taking ownership, she starts blaming and finger-pointing. She shifts responsibility to others.

"No one has it all together," she objects. "I bet if I went into any of the teachers' rooms, I could find something that each and every one of them is doing wrong."

Internally, you sigh deeply. This principal doesn't seem capable of owning her mistakes. Why can't she take the input you're giving her? Why can't she self-reflect, realize that there is a problem, and work to turn it around? It's not like you're making a judgment of her character. You're just asking her to acknowledge her mistake and come up with an action plan for regaining her staff's trust.

As a superintendent, you're very disappointed.

But how many times have you done the exact same thing without realizing it? When it's your mistake instead of someone else's, isn't it easy to rationalize and defend your choices? When someone confronts you, you tell them all the valid reasons you did what you did!

It's very difficult to humbly accept feedback, acknowledge the part you played in the problem, and work towards change. If you've ever responded like this principal, hopefully you took time to reflect and change your attitude. Hopefully you turned it around and developed a plan to change your approach. Ideally, you owned it and apologized: "My reaction was off the cuff, off the hip. I should not have reacted that way. I apologize for that."

Owning our mistakes, whether sooner or later, takes courage and bravery. But without it, your superiors and your followers will lose their respect in you. They will wonder why you're not able to learn from your failures. They'll ask themselves why you're not willing to develop strategies to continually improve. They'll think that you don't have what it takes to own your mistakes and form a plan.

MAKING IT AUTOMATIC

Ideally, practice this skill until it becomes automatic and intrinsic. When someone presents feedback, learn to respond right away in humility. Ask yourself an important question: "What role did I play in this?"

Saying, "I had nothing to do with this problem" is a cop-out. As a leader, you played a role in this somehow. You must own it at the deepest level. If you know you are part of the problem, then you can be part of solution. If you can say, "I played a part in causing this disaster," then you will begin to see the role you can play in improving the situation. You'll be equipped to develop a plan to get out of this mess.

To make this response a knee-jerk reaction, practice owning your mistakes every day. Remind yourself that every step of the way, you are likely failing in some big or small way. There will always be mistakes in your approach, priorities, or reactions. There is always something you have done that is not good enough. There's never a day when you can't find ways to improve.

This way, when someone points out a specific way you're failing, it shouldn't come as a surprise. Instead, acknowledge to yourself, "Yep, I made a mistake. I do that daily. No big deal. I will choose to learn from my mistake." When you take time to reflect, you will see the way you can contribute to the betterment of your organization.

TAKING RESPONSIBILITY

In their book, *Extreme Ownership,* Jocko Willink and Leif Babin share their experiences leading the Navy SEALS. They explain that a key part of leadership is taking responsibility for your actions—and the actions of your team. After a devastating episode of friendly fire, Jocko Willink gathered his troops together. He asked them who was at fault for the tragic event. As each officer came forward and admitted their part in the deaths, Willink refused to accept their admission. Instead, he himself took full responsibility for the lack of leadership he had shown which ultimately caused each officer to make mistakes.

Reflecting on this experience, Willink says,

> As the commander, everything that happened on the battlefield was my responsibility. *Everything.* If a supporting unit didn't do what we needed it to do, then I hadn't given clear instructions. If one of my machine gunners engaged targets outside his field of fire, then I had not ensured he understood where his field of fire was. If the enemy surprised us and hit us where we hadn't expected, then I hadn't thought through all the possibilities. No matter what, I could never blame other people when a mission went wrong.[1]

Don't misunderstand. You should never compromise your integrity, and honesty in order to back down on a decision you made. If you know you were doing right by the students you serve, there is no need to admit fault. You should never apologize for an unpopular action just to please people. Don't pretend your carefully reasoned but unwelcome decision is wrong, just because people are criticizing you.

However, there is a time and place for humility over the unavoidable mistakes you make. As a leader, you need to be able to say these difficult words in public:

"I could have done that better and I own it."
"This has been a great learning experience for me."
"In the future, I plan to do things differently."

An administrator that is excuse-driven is committing career suicide. A narcissistic finger-pointer who always says, "It's your problem, not mine," will be incapable of moving forward with his or her organization. When those behaviors exist in leadership, the administrator's career is over.

TAKING OWNERSHIP BUILDS TRUST

You may be tempted to think that you need be perfect in order to be respected by your team. Perhaps you think that admitting you did something wrong will destroy your followers' trust in you. They'll see you for who you are: incompetent, fallible, and weak.

On the contrary, admitting your mistakes is one of the most powerful ways to build trust with the teachers and staff in your building or district. Michelle Reina, author of *Trust and Betrayal in the Workplace,* shares, "In our experience, when you admit you've made a mistake, you don't erode trust in your leadership, you strengthen it. Here's why: authenticity fuels trust."[2] Tell the truth, be honest, and take ownership for the disasters that you may have contributed to.

When leaders refuse to take ownership for their problems, trust dissolves in the organization. When people see their administrator casting blame, or (even worse) ignoring the blatant problems in the organization, they will want to purchase the first ticket out of town. It's a leader's denial of responsibility—not their honest authenticity—that actually drives people away.

When your employees see their leaders as humble and responsible people, they will truly respect and want to perform for their supervisors. They will recognize that you are a leader who really gets it. They'll see that you are willing to take one for the team. They'll be more willing to get behind you, no matter what you do.

USE YOUR FAILURE TO INSPIRE

Maybe you know what it's like to work for leaders that just love to talk about themselves and their accolades. In many buildings, the administrator's self-aggrandizement has become a running joke. Teachers know they are going to have to sit through another management meeting and listen to the leader talk about their personal accomplishments and years of success. Everyone in the room looks at each other with a deep glaze over their eyes, basically saying without saying, "Here we go again . . . "

How powerful would it be if leaders would begin to talk about their failures rather than their successes? How would talking about personal failures and resilience change the narrative for these teachers? What if you shared a story of your failures and how you used them to improve as a leader? Most likely, your subordinates' respect would shoot through the roof.

Think about the most inspirational leaders who have made the greatest impact in their careers. What makes them so dynamic? What makes them stand out? What makes them light a fire in their organizations? Often, it's a willingness to be honest and learn from their mistakes.

These leaders know they are far from perfect, so they are far from prideful. Instead, they show up. They fail. They own it. They move on. They improve. They talk about their mistakes. They reason with others who have screwed up. They give grace because God knows they have needed it in so many situations.

This sounds amazing on the surface. It's easy to assent to it mentally. But when the rubber hits the road, how do leaders implement authenticity? How can you practically create an environment where it is easy to speak honestly and vulnerably about your failures?

Go back to the basics. Think about your leadership team meeting agendas. Do they lend themselves to creating a safe environment where you and your team can discuss failures and problem solve together? Or do the agendas lead to simply discussing what is going well? The key to continuous improvement is to be able to identify problems, admit shortcomings, and use a professional team to form a plan together.

When you as a leader own your mistakes, your followers will gain courage and vulnerability to follow the same example. Your teachers will be empowered to take risks, make mistakes, and openly take responsibility when things go awry. Wouldn't it be refreshing if each of your teachers and subordinates humbly admitted their role in the mistakes and failures that played out each day in your organization? It all starts with your example.

TAKE OWNERSHIP OF THE PEOPLE YOU HIRE

At times, you can legitimately say that what happened in your school or district was not your fault. You communicated as well as could be reasonably expected. You made your expectations clear. You practiced rounding and gave power to the teachers. But they still chose to deliberately defy your guidelines and strike out on their own. In this case, can't you honestly admit that it was not your fault?

Perhaps. But there is often more to the story. Did you hire this person? Did you choose to retain him or her in the organization, year after year? If so, you need to take ownership of the fact that you allowed this teacher to remain in your school. Taking ownership starts with mindset, which starts with hiring right. What are the hiring practices in your organization?

When interviewing a potential teacher or staff member, make sure you dig deep and ask questions about the individual's character. Any organization can ask typical questions about qualifications. These facts are already visible via application and resume. Often, you will need to look beneath the surface to find out the individuals' true capacity.

Why not ask your potential new hires to bring a meaningful artifact to the interview? This object or memento can give the panel a good idea of who the potential staff member is as a person. This genius idea not only communicates a desire to truly get to know the person on the other side of the interview table, but also gives you a window into the most important aspects of all: the person's character and mindset.

Pride yourself on asking deep questions or assigning unique tasks that will help you get to the root of the person's character and mindset. As you do, you will set your school apart from the norm. You'll become a leader who truly takes ownership for every person you bring into the building and every teacher that joins your team.

ADMIT ERROR WITH WISDOM, CAUTION, AND CARE

When you admit your failures, don't do so indiscriminately. Your goal is not to just plaster the information about your weaknesses on anyone who will listen. You want to make sure you don't come across as insecure and incapable, like the principal in the beginning of this chapter. Your motive in sharing your weakness is not to ask for reassurance or sympathy from your colleagues or subordinates. It's not to get other people to to sympathize with you.

Instead, make sure your recognition of failure is pointed, specific, and detailed. Include the ways you plan to improve in the future. "I feel sad that I took up so much of your valuable time with my rambling during the meeting yesterday. I value your time as teachers and educators. Next time, I will plan to end the meeting on time." Try using the nonviolent communication rubric of "I feel . . . because I did . . . because I value . . . Next time, I will . . . "[3]

In addition, because of your high-standing position, it's important to admit your failures in such a way that protects you, the school, and the district. You may need to consult with legal counsel depending on the severity to ensure your apology message will not backfire on the organization. Attorneys will advise you on the most appropriate time for a statement to the community. They will also help you draft the statement. The money spent on legal counsel is never a regrettable investment to the district.

Resilience grows as you recalibrate after failures and losses. When you are honest with yourself and others about your past and current missteps, you grow into a stronger leader. You recognize the cause-and-effect relationship of how your actions contributed to either the success or failure of the organization, and you're able to verbalize that to others. Leaders who point fingers, blame others, and make excuses will soon crumble under the pressures of leadership. But those who learn to admit their mistakes will grow in resilience and maturity.

THE TRUE NORTH

Owning your mistakes is one of the most powerful actions you can take as a leader. Humility means recognizing your mistakes and failures and knowing that there will be many more to come. Throw pride out the window, and be willing to embrace the planning and action required for change. John Maxwell said, "A man must be big enough to admit his mistakes, smart enough to profit from them, and strong enough to correct them."

The beauty is that you are given endless opportunities to make it right for students and staff that you serve. Call it Failing Forward. Call it Vulnerability. Call it Humility. Or call it Owning It. Make a commitment to pause, reflect, and recognize your contributions to the areas that need attention in your district. You will not regret taking the time to do so. Your courage will pay dividends for many years to come.

NOTES

1. Jocko Willink and Leif Babin, *Extreme Ownership: How U.S. Navy Seals Lead and Win,* (New York: St. Martin's Press, 2017), 35.

2. Michelle Reina, "How Leaders Build Trust, One Mistake at a Time," *Reina Trust Building,* Accessed November 29, 2021, https://reinatrustbuilding.com/how-leaders-build-trust-one-mistake-at-a-time/.

3. "Nonviolent Communication - M. Rosenberg (summary)," Last modified December 1, 2015, Accessed November 23, 2021, https://www.mudamasters.com/en/personal-growth-effectiveness/nonviolent-communication-mrosenberg-summary.

Chapter 5

The U Word

Surviving and Thriving during Union Negotiations

Union. What are the first thoughts that come to your mind when you hear the U-word? Drawn out negotiations? Grievances? Unfair treatment? Feeling like you are handcuffed to employees who are resistant to change?

For many leaders, the word "Union" brings rolled eyes and long sighs followed by anxiety and sleepless nights. The term "Union" is almost a bad word in public education.

When you embarked into the world of administration, you heard the rumors.

"The Union wants to keep bad teachers employed."
"The Union only cares about pay raises."
"The Union is a true force to be reckoned with."

Everyone can agree that the Union often makes continuous demands of administrators. It's natural to feel fearful and scared of these powerful negotiators. You go into administration vowing to never have your own nasty run in with them. Ever.

Because of this bad rap, the advice you are going to hear next is going to surprise you. It will shock you and may rub you the wrong way. But it goes straight to the point, because it's true. Here it is:

Partner with the Union.

Say what?

Yes, partner with the Union. The thing you fear the most is the thing you must embrace with open arms. True vulnerability means showing up and engaging with others, even when you're afraid.

No matter how uncomfortable it may be, it is important to embrace the Union's role and purpose. Don't just go through the motions. Do not fake it.

Know that the Union can in fact be your biggest advocate. You must prioritize forming solid and authentic relationships with these valuable partners.

"Embrace their role and purpose? Exactly what *is* their purpose?" you may ask.

Most educators know that the purpose of the Union is to set standard operating procedures for teachers, certified workers, bus drivers, and lunchroom monitors. Every class of worker has their own Union group, and most districts have an agreement with each of them.

Typically, the Union says, "OK district, these are the terms of our employment. This is the number of hours we are going to work. This is our pay, and this is how much we want you to contribute to our health insurance." But everyone knows it is all negotiable, and the district leaders immediately propose counter terms. The haggling goes back and forth until everyone finally comes to an agreement.

Often, the relationship between the district and the union is very adversarial. The union can sometime begin by coming forward with crazy, unreasonable demands on behalf of their members. "We are asking for a 13% pay increase to make up for the years of flat funding."

The district representative then retorts, "How dare you think that we can afford that? I don't even know why you think we can do that. It's crazy."

That's when things can turn ugly. Hostility sometimes reigns through the negotiation process. Nine times out of ten, it's a fight. Animosity builds over time. Leaders are just so disgusted with the demands that the union leaders put on the table. They don't even try to hide their offense and anger.

During Union negotiations, both sides make back and forth requests until there's an agreement. It doesn't always happen quickly. Depending on how crazy the demands are, the process can last months and even years often requiring the assistance of county or state Union intervention.

Though you wish you could hide your head in the sand and skip the Union meetings all together, it's impossible to avoid them. Instead, equip yourself with the tools you'll need to be successful.

GET TO KNOW YOUR UNION LEADER

Administrators need to be mindful of what Union leaders want and need. Attend local and state Union-sponsored events so you can truly understand their mindset and initiatives. Rather than make assumptions about their motives and desires, take the time to hear them out.

It's true, you'd rather not think about the Union. It's easy to let their demands and desires slide out of your visual field, because you'd rather pretend the Union doesn't exist. Instead of dealing with this problem, you focus on becoming a better leader. You attend workshops designed for new administrators. You busy yourself with non-Union issues: your administrative association, your PD classes and support groups, your studying new research.

All these items are good, but they must not replace the uncomfortable task of getting to know the Union members. It's critical to become super immersed as fast as you can in the Union vibe. You need to keep your finger on the pulse of the Union. Know their demands and potential requests.

In education, there is no escaping the Union. In some states, the teacher's union funds many of the legislature's campaigns. People in the community will have a strong sense of political loyalty to the Union's ideas and initiatives. Legislators will often support Union opinions. The influence of big city Unions reaches even to rural areas, since the state laws apply to all districts. With the powerful impact that the Union has, it is best to seek to understand what they have to say. You don't necessarily have to embrace and agree, but you must be fully aware and compassionate to their views. That way, you will be able to navigate the waters of legislative change.

One of the best ways to do this is to get to know the Union Leaders in your area. You'll need to get to know site leaders, as well as district leaders. In short, site union leaders are the lower-level leaders who meet with the staff in a certain building to get their feedback. They then take that information to the top.

The president of the union oversees all the schools, listening to the feedback from the site Union leaders. They were elected, appointed, or nominated as the president or chair, and they are most often part of the negotiation process with the district. Sometimes, they bring to the table the site leaders as well, depending on how big the district is.

One of the best ways to get to know your Union leaders is to take them out to dinner. You and your Union leader may be very different, but over shared food, you often will find common ground. You will bond over shared memories and laugh over differences. You'll relish your shared joy of food—even though she prefers boiled peanuts, and you prefer the hard, crunchy ones! You'll spend time together at the neighborhood bar and grill scraping those plates clean as you agree on what appetizers to order for your dinner. Most of all, you'll learn to admire your leader's good qualities—stubbornness, work ethic, passion for learning, and fighting for what is right.

It's important to see these Union leaders as real human beings. Before the big day of negotiations, spend time getting to know them as people. Spending time with them will also humanize yourself to them as well. It will be harder to attack each other when you've laughed over martinis.

When you least expect it, you will learn more from these Union members than you ever thought imaginable. Your Union leader can become your partner, technology coach, colleague, and friend. Will you always see things eye to eye? Absolutely not. But can you respect each other? Absolutely yes. Your union leader may serve in many union leadership roles in your district. You can walk along them through many years.

Your union leader is an advocate for your state's Union teacher association, while you are focused primarily on your state's non-Union administrative association. In many legislative policies, those two are not in agreement. But you need to take the time to recognize that you both care deeply about student and staff issues. You and your union leader can earn respect with your colleagues as you both travel near and far to learn and serve as a voice for those you represent back at home.

In short, your goal is to build teamwork based on trust and good communication. Your purpose should be to form a respectful, effective partnership with the union. As you get to know the Union leaders, you can gain camaraderie that will prepare you for difficult times ahead.

BE PREPARED

You can't escape the annual negotiation process. The only thing you can do is try your best to be prepared. As a district administrator, you must understand the district budget in order to effectively negotiate with the union. Armed with a thorough knowledge of the budget, a good leader can assertively tell the Union what the district *can* do. Rather than falling into negative communication patterns, the leader clearly outlines what's realistic.

Leaders are often unprepared for union negotiations. When that's the case, they're unable to see the big picture during negotiations with the union. When the Union representative comes in with an outlandish demand, the unprepared leader has nowhere to turn.

"We want a 13% raise, we want two less work days, we want more prep time, we want . . . we want . . . we want. . . ." The Union rep's eyes are flashing. As you listen to his requests, you see his face like a prey sees his predator. He is just so angry and mean. His voice is stone cold. He's a predator ready to attack, a lion ready to eat its meal. The room is spinning.

You sit there in shock. Opening your mouth, you stammer, "What? Why would you even ask that?"

You know that there's no way that your budget can support that 13% raise. But because you haven't thoroughly prepared for the meeting, you have no idea what to say next.

As a district admin, you are freaking out on the inside. Immediately, you go on the defensive. You know you are the prey, and you have nowhere to turn. You're just trying to escape this attacking lion.

Now you realize how important it is to research the budget and financial situation ahead of time. You can count on it, the Union is going to throw out something unattainable to start the negotiation. As a leader, you need to be ready to throw out something more reasonable, explaining why the first figure isn't reasonable. You need to know the budget like the back of your hand.

Now, when the union blurts out, "Our members want at 13% pay raise," you're prepared with your comeback. Because you've done your research, you know for a fact that there's no way the district can afford more than 5%.

You assertively respond, "How about 3.5%. We can definitely work with that."

They'll say, "Come on. We know you can afford more than that."

You reply, "Let me show you the books. We can afford only 4–5% max. Next year, if things are good, we can offer you an additional raise."

Instead of running away or attacking back try to rationalize. There's an art and craft to doing this, and it's very difficult. This leads to our next step: the importance of learning and practicing negotiation.

LEARN NEGOTIATION SKILLS

Negotiation day is a day that most administrators dread all year long. That's why it's so important to deal with this issue straightforwardly. You can't avoid negotiation day, so you must face it head on.

Rather than defaulting to an adversarial relationship, you must learn to negotiate with skill and respect. It's important to develop a culture where the leaders of the district can maintain a calm, non-confrontational attitude. They must listen openly to the demands, then be prepared to offer alternative, realistic terms.

Just hearing the word "negotiations" leads to eye rolling and increased heart rate. But again, this topic goes back to mindset. If you think about negotiations from a different perspective, you can actually look forward to them for one reason: progress. Not necessarily agreement, but progress towards moving in the right direction.

Remain super calm and have your ducks in the row before you get into that room. Know what your approach is going to be. Anticipate what the opponents are going to put on the table.

In his book, *Never Split the Difference,* Chris Voss teaches key negotiating skills that have worked with the most hardened of kidnappers. He says that before the negotiation, it's important to be clear about what you want. He suggests, "Think through best case and worst-case scenarios, but only write down the specific goal that represents the best case." Clearly defined goals, he says, "end up getting better deals."[1] Think objectively about what you want, as well as what the other person wants.[2] Define mentally what you are "trying to accomplish," and why it is important to you.[3] How about the Union members? What are their goals and values, and what are they up against?

As you enter negotiations, don't be overly pessimistic or optimistic. Be prepared for anything. Sometimes, you will be pleasantly surprised. You'll say to yourself, "Wow. I thought they were going to be asking for a lot more. We can actually do this." Other times, it's the opposite. "Wow. That was a scary situation where I had to work my way out of their demands."

Most of all, stay open minded. Voss says, "Never be so sure of what you want that you wouldn't take something better. Once you've got flexibility in the forefront of your mind you come into negotiation with a winning mindset."[4] When you maintain an open heart towards your own needs and the needs of the Union, teachers, and staff, you will be poised and prepared for a successful negotiation day.

Even if you are working for a non-union organization, the approach is the same. There may not be a contract, but there are still staff desires and concerns that you'll need to take into consideration. There are still important opportunities to truly listen and engage in healthy conversation. There have been times when a district negotiation team will actually tell the county union liaison (who can also be frightening) in so many words where to stick it, especially if the county union rep is stalling progress or making unnecessary statements and requests.

Negotiation also provides an opportunity for you to voice your disagreement with the contents of the contract. Rather than complaining and griping about the content of the contract, take your chance to voice these concerns through the negotiation process.

In summary, keep your head on straight, stay calm, and keep your goal in mind. Negotiation day will come and go, and with the skills and tools you've learned, you have a high chance of being successful. You've got this.

MAINTAINING DISCIPLINE

There's an underlying question that many administrators struggle with during the early years: "How do I advocate for students and good teaching when there are some teachers on staff who raise the Union flag every time I challenge them?" Every time you bring up an area of improvement or inconvenience, the teacher references their contract.

For example, when you ask staff to stay a few minutes after school for a meeting, the site union rep reminds you of the hours of the workday outlined in their contract. You roll out instructional coaching, asking staff to be open to instructional feedback, but teachers respond that the coach is not welcome.

As per contract the only feedback is through formal administrative observation and evaluation.

You ask staff to make sure they are making contact regularly with parents to inform them of students' academic progress, and they state that this mandate is not in the contract. Say what? Since when is consistent parent communication an irrational request?

At this point, some administrators easily succumb to embracing an Us versus Them approach. They say, "This is going to be a battle that I will fight." Even though this happens all of the time, it only has a disastrous outcome.

Instead, think of creative approaches that can motivate the staff to do the same healthy habits, without a direct confrontation. Did you notice that each statement above started with, "You asked staff to. . . . "? What if you were not the one that asked? What if the staff asked each other to follow through with these same initiatives? That would make your job a lot more pleasant. It would align with the leadership perspective that states that staff must obey initiatives and buy in to change.

You could start by forming a leadership team composed of highly respected teachers—not just by administration but by their colleagues. The key person to have on the team is your site Union representative. Why? You need that challenge and perspective. And you also need to have the ability to troubleshoot ahead of time before it becomes a "Union issue."

If your leadership team is full of "yes people," this will still result in revolt. These "yes men" do not have what it takes to justify the cause to the people in the organization. Don't fill your leadership team with friends. Fill it with amazing leaders with whom you do not always agree. This will result in healthy conversations and debates, and it will definitely keep you learning.

Of course, this is not to say that every ill-prepared and untalented teacher should remain in the classroom. But as you navigate these difficult waters, it's important to get on the same team with the Union. No matter what, don't act out of fear. The concept of teacher tenure is so much more difficult to maneuver when the approach is Us versus Them, so focus on partnering with the Union in deciding whether a certain teacher needs to continue in her position.

It's difficult when a teacher has an instantly observable lack of classroom management and student engagement. You can tell that not much teaching is going on in her room, and a lot of crazy student behaviors are happening. When you question the teacher or provide feedback, the response is to blame the students, the parents, and the external factors that neither of you can control. What should you do?

Perhaps you adore this teacher outside of the classroom. You know her heart is solid, and she truly wants to be successful. You also know she is just as disappointed with the learning outcomes as you are. But it is difficult to have a conversation with this teacher without her requesting union presence.

Instead of giving in to fear, you ask the teacher an important question: "What do you need to be successful?"

Both of you know that firing the students is not an option. Neither is firing the parents. The teacher is the one who must change, but your role is not to attack her. Your job is truly to listen to this brave individual who is on the front lines each and every day. You must absolutely acknowledge the very real challenges of the extreme student behaviors and the traumas that these students bring into the classrooms. You must be sensitive to the instructional staff that are truly trying their hardest to make a difference. How do you do this? Not just by saying, "I get it," but through action. Provide tools and practical support systems to help your teacher improve.

In addition, bring the Union rep into the process earlier rather than later. You must first abandon the mindset that tells you that the Union is out to get you. Instead, you invite the Union rep into your office to discuss the struggles and concerns you've had with this teacher. You meet regularly over coffee outside of work, you laugh together, you vent together, and you demonstrate that you are absolutely on the same team.

This all goes back to swallowing pride, putting personal agendas aside, and embracing the idea that leaders can only take an organization as far as the organization wants to go. As a leader, principal, or superintendent, you are the facilitator of change. But you are not the one who ultimately directs change. The Union serves a very real purpose of working side by side administration to accomplish agreed upon goals and at the same time ensuring teachers have the assurances that are outlined in the contract.

At the end of the day, you as a leader want your people taken care of. Even more so, you want them to want to work with you. Sure, you may have been so blunt to tell a teacher that perhaps teaching is not for them. That does not go against any contract. Perhaps you've made the teacher tearful and angry throughout that process. You and your union leader can both agree on a foundational principle: there are just some educators who should not be in the classroom.

By partnering with the Union representative early in the process, dynamic leaders can steer the employee in a different direction with Union support. This should ultimately be done with class, dignity, and compassion. Don't wait until the spring deadline to suddenly say, "You are a non-re-elect." This approach shows complete disrespect.

Sure, legally per contract the staff member may not need to be offered a reason for their termination. But early and honest feedback is what sets apart mediocre leaders from great leaders. Learn the ability to guide staff early on, providing honest feedback so that the ultimate release is not a complete shock to one's soul. Your staff members deserve to know the areas they could improve upon, and they also deserve the time to reflect and try to improve.

THE TRUE NORTH

The admin and Union partnership can sometimes be messy, complicated, and downright frustrating for both. However, never forget that in many ways, your relationship with the Union is like any other partnership. It's simply a process of working together, overcoming obstacles, and learning an insane amount from one other.

With some hard work and intentionality, you can form a good relationship with your Union leader. You can actually look forward to your monthly dinner dates outside of work—not because you have to, but because you choose to. Recognize that you both want amazing opportunities for the students you serve through your different organizations. Focus on how exciting it is to hear about ways to make this happen! You can authentically value your union leader's perspective. Without a doubt, you can both agree that the pretzel bites and tacos are a perfect meal choice after a long, hard day.

NOTES

1. Chris Voss, *Never Split the Difference,* (New York City: Harper Business, 2016), 253.

2. Ibid., 256.

3. Ibid.

4. Ibid., 252–53.

Chapter 6

Passed Up

Rebounding after Career Disappointment

"When one door closes, another door opens." You've probably heard this old saying throughout your career. And you may even believe it. But when it is your turn for the door to be slammed hard in your face, the pain lasts. For a very long time.

No matter how hard you try to avoid it, no leader can escape the very real challenge of being Passed Up. Whether you are a leader that has served in your current organization the past 30+ years, a new leader who plans to stay 30 more years, or a person who seeks out frequent district change, you will eventually experience the pain and betrayal of being passed over.

Most likely, you'll be passed up when everyone was convinced the position was yours. You will be passed up when the community appeared to be standing behind you. Worst of all, you could be passed up when you gave your heart and soul into obtaining that next promotion.

When this tragic situation happens to you, your friends and family attempt to console you. Even though you appreciate their words, their comforting gestures can be downright annoying. Quite frankly, there are no words that can make it better. There is no option but to go through the healing process—a true type of grieving.

GRIEF AND RESILIENCE

Perhaps you've recently experienced being Passed Up. It is still fresh. And at times, it still makes you angry. If this is you, you must own your pain so that you can make the choice as to just *how* to move forward. You cannot just sit back and say, "I am thankful for this experience," meanwhile refusing to take action. Instead, it's time to get back in the game. The courage to try again involves an insane amount of vulnerability, because you are taking the risk that you may in fact be Passed Up again.

Ever heard the quote by Theodore Roosevelt about trying and failing? We're all familiar with it:

> The credit belongs to the man who is actually in the arena, whose face is marred by dust and sweat and blood; who strives valiantly; who errs, who comes short again and again, . . . who knows great enthusiasms, the great devotions; who spends himself in a worthy cause; who at the best knows in the end the triumph of high achievement, and who at the worst, if he fails, at least fails while daring greatly, so that his place shall never be with those cold and timid souls who neither know victory nor defeat.[1]

You understand the appeal of these words on paper. But after you've known the great enthusiasm and the great devotion yourself? After you've spent yourself in a worthy cause that you felt we were highly qualified for? And after you've "come up short" in the eyes of those who should have applauded you? You might start wishing you belonged to those cold and timid souls who didn't try.

Brené Brown explains that shame is a close companion to those who risk, try hard to achieve something, and are nonetheless rejected. She says,

> If we want to be able to move through the difficult disappointments, the hurt feelings, and the heartbreaks that are inevitable in a fully lived life, we can't equate defeat with being unworthy of love, belonging, and joy. If we do, we'll never show up and try again. Shame hangs out in the parking lot of the arena, waiting for us to come out defeated and determined to never take risks. It laughs and says, "I told you this was a mistake. I knew you weren't enough." Shame resilience is the ability to say, "This hurts. This is disappointing, maybe even devastating. But success and recognition and approval are not the values that drive me. My value is courage, and I was just courageous. You can move on, shame."[2]

This courage doesn't come easily. It's born in the crucible of difficult experiences. Let's imagine a scenario of being passed up that is familiar to all leaders. Let's find out how to rise strong from the ashes and continue to have the courage to risk.

The most painful situation of all comes from personal, undeserved betrayal. It's plenty disappointing to be Passed Up as the external candidate who is competing for a job along with hundreds of other candidates. That experience can be wildly disheartening and depressing. But the true sting comes from being groomed to be the next principal, director, CBO, or superintendent.

When the plan just does not work out, despite your personal and professional investments, you feel that you have been personally betrayed by those who had all but promised you the position.

You've worked towards your goal for many long and arduous years. Perhaps you've served in the same district for decades: first as a reading specialist, then as a teacher, assistant principal, principal, and finally an assistant superintendent. You worked your ass off to get the assistant superintendent job. It was not handed to you: there were several candidates, multiple interviews, and a long waiting period to find out if you were the Chosen One. Even though you were the internal candidate of choice, you knew the competition would be steep. You purchased new dress suits, created a slick portfolio, and spent many hours meeting with mentors asking for interview guidance.

Then the moment of truth arrived. You will never forget getting the call. You were on yard duty at the school, or you were sitting in your office rechecking the budget. You remember the exact moment you were called to meet your superintendent over lunch to notify you of his decision.

As you hurried to meet him, your hands shaking from anxiety, you stayed true to your core values. You thought, "No matter what the outcome, I vow to remain devoted to these children, whether it is from this school site or the downtown office." Then you opened the door to the restaurant, break room, or office where you were to meet your superintendent.

Over lunch, the superintendent spoke about what he desired in a partner. He explained that his job was to ensure that you were prepared to be the next superintendent of the district. He praised your gifts and discussed areas where you needed to really focus on in order to improve. As you walked out of the restaurant that day, you were truly on top of the freaking world.

Years of preparation flew by incredibly fast. During this time, there were several highs and lows. You built your leadership confidence, took risks, and truly learned the power of vulnerability and partnership with staff and parents. You remained insanely connected to your students through classroom visits, which kept you grounded on the right work.

You were *on your way.*

But then it happened. The shot in the gut that spiraled you down to depression and forced you to a crossroads. The life-shattering experience that caused you to look inward and ask yourself, "Can I truly be at peace with being good enough for myself—even if others reject me? Am I enough, even without this position?"

Perhaps the hammer dropped suddenly, out of the blue. Or perhaps you had begun to see the handwriting on the wall. Either way, you knew this was the beginning of the end. The superintendent announced he would be moving on to other ventures, and he informed you that the board would only be entertaining internal candidates. Notice plural: *candidates.*

Your mind began to spin. *You mean there is someone else internally that is being prepared and groomed for my dream job?* You knew that during your tenure as assistant superintendent, your evaluations were glowing, your relationship with the board was stellar, and your relationship with staff and families solid. Who could be attempting to sabotage this career path? Who has put in the time to truly invest in this district long term?

Then you are informed that a colleague also had the aspiration to become the next superintendent.

You may have thought, "Ok, here we go." You knew that nothing in life comes easy, and you chose to view this as just another challenge that you were more than willing to work for.

Perhaps the biggest part of the challenge was knowing who to believe. A school board member told you that they found out about another candidate, but they would be shocked if you were not selected. You wanted to believe them, but you were not sure who to trust. You knew that what they were saying was partly true. Or maybe it was just that people wanted to give you encouragement.

Either way, truth be told you started accepting the fact that you may very well not be selected. Perhaps you observed the relationship that had been built between the other candidate and the superintendent, and you felt insecure. You knew you couldn't compete, and you debated on backing out as you started seeing the handwriting on the wall.

When you confided in your family, they may have told you, "Stay strong. The job is yours." The response of people you trusted within the district was exactly the same.

But at some point, you realized you knew better. You continued to see signs that you were not being included in "future superintendent" type of conversations. It felt as though were going into an interview in which the decision had already been made.

Even so, you determined to do your best and knocked the interview out of the park with confidence and focus. It was clear to you that if you were not offered the position, there was not anything you could have done better.

No matter the specific details of your story, you know the feeling of being Passed Up. The day of the official notice, your heart sank when you were asked to enter the meeting first. You knew that the board would want to spend the most time with the candidate who was The Chosen One. You knew you had not been selected, but you still walked into the boardroom with your head held high and sat down with the board president and vice president. This was likely one of the most pivotal moments of your lifetime.

The board president said something that you can still remember today. Something to the effect that your interview was fantastic and your experience and years with the district speak for themselves. Then that infamous long pause. " . . . Unfortunately, we cannot offer you the superintendent position." Gulp. You looked at the vice president and could tell that there was true emotion behind the solemn face. Your only response: "And I will be fine." You stood up and walked out.

Perhaps you had to cancel a celebration dinner or an evening with family. Perhaps you slid into your office and told your fiancé to cancel the celebration. Perhaps you messaged a few colleagues who were waiting for your celebratory text. Maybe you waited until most of the district office staff had left for the day until you finally walked out of the district office. Either way, it was a moment of intense difficulty for you.

Maybe you were alone in your car or you house when you finally let yourself cry. Actually scream. You were angry. You were hurt. You were confused. And yet you were not surprised. Perhaps a friend offers words of wisdom: "You will never know why and you don't want to know. Now you move on." And that is exactly what all leaders do when they are Passed Up. You grieve. And then you Move On.

Some may tell you to revolt the decision, but you know deep down that acceptance is the only option. Perhaps you choose to stay in your current position, or perhaps the experience is truly an awakening of your potential to serve somewhere else.

As you go through your own experience of being Passed Up, you can learn to thrive and not just survive. You can say more than, "I will be fine." As you experience the excruciating pain of loss and betrayal, you can come out the victor. You can honestly tell yourself and others, "I will be better off because of this. I will be happier because of this. I will keep on keeping on!"

Sure the hurt will still sting sometimes, but the lessons here are so huge. As you look back, you may realize that this experience was exactly what you needed. John Maxwell once said, "People say there are two kinds of learning: experience, which is gained from your own mistakes, and wisdom, which is learned from the mistakes of others."[3] Think of it this way: you not only learn valuable lessons for yourself, but you will also learn powerful insights that you can share with others as they travel life's difficult path.

If you have been recently passed up, here are some tips to help you reach the success you dream for—even if it looks different than you once imagined.

DEALING WITH DEPRESSION

Your first reaction may be to regroup and rebound quickly. You don't want your friends and family to see you wallowing in despair. You don't want them to think that this experience has defeated you. Maybe you'd rather have them think that it barely affected you.

Yes, the ultimate goal is to move forward with courage towards your next endeavor. But that doesn't mean that you won't face times of deep depression. When you're passed up, it can send an administrator into a really dark place. You may begin to consider, "Is this career even for me? Why did I ever pursue this job? I believe I'm in the wrong career."

Rather than doubting yourself, making drastic decisions, or putting on a strong front and pretending that nothing is wrong, you have to swallow your pride. You must face the grief head on. Admit that this experience was hard for you. Allow yourself to mourn. Enter the stages of grief. It's okay to spend some time being angry, depressed, and sad.

Focus on dispersing your anger in a healthy way, rather than a destructive way. Don't waste time yelling at your superiors, trying to control dynamics, demanding they tell you why you didn't get the position. Recognize the decision will not change. Instead of bucking the system, accept what happened. Form a new plan and go on influencing kids somewhere else where they need it.

It can take several months before you feel like yourself again. Like any process of grief recovery, it will take time. Find healing through prayer, meditation, exercise, and trust in your faith and community. Read the Bible and other uplifting books. Access the peace that passes understanding.

Soon, you may discover you have an unexplained sense of peace. You may feel like it's going to be fine, even though you don't know why. It's okay this position didn't work out. You'll realize your anger and sadness is turning into acceptance. So much growth is happening in this important process.

If you refuse to acknowledge your grief and work through it, you will enter into a longer, more drawn-out depression period. This desolate despair will waste precious time that you could have been influencing kids. It's time to face your sadness, find healing, and move on to the next career path life has for you.

CREATE A FLEXIBLE CAREER PLAN

When the going gets tough, you will need a plan. It's best if you've made that plan years in advance. You should be ready for a Plan A, but also have Plans B, C, and D prepared. That way, when the worst-case scenario happens, you don't waste time in directionless apathy. You'll know exactly where you're headed next. After the grief period is over, you can spend time headed towards your dreams instead of wandering around in confusion.

Your plan needs to look at the big picture. Ask yourself, "In which job or career do I foresee myself when I retire? Where do I want to end my career? As a principal? As a district superintendent?"

Your end goal makes a difference. Some people want to go into administration at a young age. Others seek administration as a third or fourth career. Your timeline and plan will be different, depending on how much time you have available to devote to preparing for administration. Your end goal affects the way you seek out varying networking opportunities. It affects the timing of making connections and finding available positions.

Once you've decided on your end goal, work backward from there. If your end goal is to retire at 60, perhaps you calculate that you have 30 until retirement. Given that fact, what is your trajectory? If you're aiming to be a superintendent, you must understand the career path trajectory to reach that goal. You must move from assistant principal to principal to assistant superintendent. You aim for the district office and applying for the superintendent position.

As this chapter has already discussed, your goals don't always unfold as planned. Understanding the path and trajectory is great, but your plans don't always work the way you intended. Along what seems to be a 100% certain, guaranteed pathway, you may be passed up. Another candidate may be chosen as a better leader for whatever reason. That's where Plan B comes in.

After the disappointment, you have to regroup. You'll take time to reflect: "What is the matter with me? Why am I not good enough?" You'll feel disillusioned. But then you'll have a choice to make. You can either stay in a very depressed state, or go back and revive and revise your career plan.

If you have already considered Plans B, C, and D, you can easily reconfigure and keep pressing forward. You'll say to yourself, "My goal is still to be a superintendent. How can I still make that happen in another district? How many years do I have left? Now I only have 20 years left. In these 20 years, how can I be on the lookout for positions to get me to my ultimate goal?"

It's important to keep this flexible plan in the forefront of your mind. There are always schools and districts looking for new leadership. Schools and districts get burnt out on their administrators just as quickly as administrators get burnt out on schools and district. You rarely see a principal stay for 30 years at the same school. Most only stay a maximum of three to five years. Staff get burned out quickly and are always looking for a fresh face. That fresh face could be you! Just because you're passed up in your district doesn't mean you can't find a new challenge, a new place, and new students in a new district. Perhaps you'll even recognize that you're burnt out in your district and are grateful for a revised plan and a new start.

Ask yourself these questions:

- What is your ultimate career goal in school and/or district administration?
- When do you want to accomplish this goal by?
- What positions are necessary to obtain in the interim to be qualified to obtain the ultimate position?
- What other options do you have if your original career plan fails?
- What alternative plans do you have for your advancement?

Always keep in mind your Plan B. There are always new horizons available. You just have to seek them.

SEE THE BENEFITS

Although it may be difficult to see the benefits right away, you will eventually realize that your experience of rejection has not been wasted. Being passed up gives you invaluable experiences that will serve you well in the future.

First, being passed up will give you interview experience that will serve you well when you apply for future positions. In the overarching scheme of things, realize that your application process for one failed job attempt is simply a steppingstone towards the successful position you'll get in the future. Each failed attempt is a practice run towards the dream job you will eventually win.

Have a growth mindset, a positive outlook that views every mistake as an opportunity for learning. As you approach another job opportunity, realize that it can't hurt anything to try. Sure, applying for administration is a highly competitive process. You don't know the pool of applicants, and you have no idea if your experience and qualifications are going to be enough for the board. But what can it hurt to try?

Instead of focusing on potential failure and another painful loss, focus on the learning experiences you will gain. You will go through another interview with the board, where you will again have the opportunity to practice. It's just like a rehearsal. Every interview is a rehearsal for the main job you will one day be offered. You will have learned the type of questions they ask. You will learn how to manage your emotions and body language in front of powerful people. You can apply this information to the next interview. You'll continue to hone the art and craft of interviewing well. You'll always get the experience of the interview, even if you don't get the job.

Second, being passed up gives you the valuable opportunity to share with others down the road. You can share your story of rejection and resilience with people in your sphere. Everyone can relate to rejection in one sphere or another. This doesn't just apply to fellow administrators or school employees. Anyone, young or old, can benefit from the stories you have to share. Your message of courage and hope can help others to rebound after loss, find a new path when the first one is blocked, and to keep trying for their dreams.

More specifically, your story can bring courage to other administrators or teachers hoping to go into administration. As you go through this heart-breaking experience, other administrators are watching. Their eyes are on you. How are you going to react? There are two words that come out: class and dignity. When they see the confidence, class, and dignity with which you move forward, they'll start to contact you and ask for help with processing their own experiences. They'll use your story to give them courage to try again. You'll be able to reach out to struggling administrators and say, "Hey, look, listen, this is going to be fine."

Leaders must have the courage to talk more about these experiences so that they can help others who are in the same situation. Ask yourself why you are holding back on sharing your setbacks. Why is there shame in admitting to not being the chosen one? Don't be so prideful that you forget to recognize an important fact: even during your low points, you have a tremendous sphere of influence.

Misery loves company. As you reach out to other administrators, you each share your war stories. "We were excited about that opportunity, we lost it, but we'll have another one down the road. We've got this." The mentorship and coaching you can provide for other disappointed administrators can be invaluable.

BE REALISTIC

If you are on the road to becoming an administrator, know that being Passed Up is part of the journey. You might as well start mentally preparing now. John Maxwell said, "Don't buy into the notion that mistakes can somehow be avoided. They can't be."[4] Failure, disappointment, and rejection are inevitable.

Don't waste time beating yourself up and wondering what you could have done differently. Instead, focus on how you can move forward from here. John Maxwell has famously said, "'Failing forward' is the ability to get back up after you've been knocked down, learn from your mistake, and move forward in a better direction."[5]

As you prepare for your long-term career goals, it's important to honestly look reality in the face. There will be rejection and disappointment along the way. But you can both survive and thrive, get back up again, and keep going!

THE TRUE NORTH

As administrators, "we're all in this together." Most administrators are passed up at one time or another. It's common to apply for jobs and not get them. It's normal to think you have it in the hat, to think it is a guarantee, but then to have the carpet pulled out from underneath you. The shock factor is devastating. It's embarrassing to watch your community and family be stunned and disappointed alongside you.

But being passed up may be the only way to get to the humbling point of seeking necessary career change. Like a sailboat on the sea, you must simply adjust your sails and take off in a new direction. The secret is truly accepting the darkest and coldest of days. Without the rough seas, the sails can't be adjusted. And adjusting the sails is the only way to experience the beautiful journey.

NOTES

1. Theodore Roosevelt, in Erin McCarthy, "Roosevelt's 'The Man in the Arena,'" *Mental Floss,* Last modified April 23, 2020, Accessed December 2, 2021, https://www.mentalfloss.com/article/63389/roosevelts-man-arena.

2. Brown, Brené, *Daring Greatly*, 67.

3. John Maxwell, *Failing Forward: How to Make the Most of Your Mistakes,* (Nashville: Thomas Nelson, 2007) as quoted on Goodreads, Accessed December 2, 2021, https://www.goodreads.com/work/quotes/614412-failing-forward?page=2.

4. Ibid.

5. Ibid.

Chapter 7

The Pandemic Pivot

Learning Flexibility and Strength in the Face of Disaster

In 2020, administration faced a learning experience like no other. It was an opportunity to internalize the most important leadership lessons ever. What was that life-changing learning opportunity? The global COVID-19 pandemic.

No one escaped the trials, burdens, decisions, and stress of the pandemic. In the crucible of a worldwide disaster, leaders learned lessons that strengthened them to face challenges in an ever-changing world. These lessons can now be shared with others, as these general principles can be applied to any major disaster or disruption that comes your way. Any crisis—a school shooting, a natural disaster, or any other danger—requires the same intense level of discipline, care, and communication.

THE DISASTER UNFOLDS

In March of 2020, many schools around the country were completely blindsided by news of a new virus from China. Going home for spring break, kids and teachers expected to resume as normal after a week of fun in the sun. But just like that, everything shut down. Life as people knew it had come to an end.

Initially, schools planned to reopen shortly, providing various instructional options for families. But before long, teachers were faced with the fact that school was not going to be the same for a very long time. Districts and state governments mandated distance learning for all. Immediately, thousands of teachers had to pivot to remote teaching, experimenting with online interfaces they had never used before.

One week, schools were normal. The next week, schools were a ghost town. One day, teachers hoped to have students back by the end of spring break. The next, they were facing a long, bleak corridor of online learning that seemed to never end.

Board of Education meetings happened every few weeks, always issuing ever-changing ideas, plans, and mandates. Teachers tried to prepare for everything at the same time. Promises of reopening, threats of closing, and everything in between boomeranged off the walls of teachers' minds. No one knew what was happening. Who knows what the mandates would be by next week?

Teachers and administrators felt like they were going absolutely crazy; there is no other way to put it. To say the process was an emotional roller coaster and produced complete exhaustion is an understatement. Every day, administrators felt like they were doing a crappy job. Every day, they experienced again the reality that "haters gonna hate." And every day, the pressure felt unbearable.

Administrators were pressured to successfully pivot and go with a different plan, depending on the reality of the virus. They were pressured to compete with other superintendents to see who would be the first one to close shop, who would be the first one to reopen, who would be the first one to adjust, and who would be the first one to go with the next educational flavor-of-the-month-plan based on the newest state guidelines. COVID created the perfect storm in which leaders were forgetting how to lead. They were rushing to make rash decisions with increasing pressures from anyone and everyone.

Unexpected, life-altering change is tough to handle. It comes out of left field when you least expect it. That's why it's important to prepare ahead of time for the worst-case scenario. The following principles are effective any time, whether things are going poorly or not. But they are especially effective during times of worldwide or citywide stress and disaster.

EFFECTIVE COMMUNICATION

Since the pandemic surfaced in spring of 2020, there has truly been only one leadership skill that makes or breaks a district. It doesn't matter how big or small the district is or whether the school is public or private. It all boils down to one key element: effective, timely communication.

During 2020, a lack of communication from administrators caused many communities to spiral out of control into a dark abyss of misery for everyone. These leaders knew exactly what they were planning. They knew what the next step of reopening schools was. If they had a plan and knew what they were doing, why couldn't the community just trust them to execute it?

Was there really a need to constantly keep the community up to date with their plans?

Experience demonstrated just how important timely communication was. When administrators failed to message staff and families or communicated very little, disaster ensued. This one mistake drove parents to form their own false realities of what was really going on. Teachers began to feel like they had zero say in the planning process. Instead of building a community of trust, administrators fostered an "Us vs. Them" culture.

On the other end of the spectrum, successful leaders took the "Communication Overload" strategy. Every day, they busted their butts calling, texting, emailing, and posting updates. Even if there was no update to be had, they communicated that reality with staff and parents. They hosted parent forums at least monthly, sometimes weekly.

Why did successful leaders take such pains to communicate with their communities? With so much information being thrown at staff and families from so many different local, state, and federal sources, parents were becoming confused. They deserved to hear from their own administrator firsthand.

No staff member or parent has ever said, "The superintendent communicates too much." It is always the exact opposite. In short, public relations during a pandemic are insanely important. It has been affirmed time and time again that this should be the number one priority. Otherwise, people will in fact make up their own truths, which are most often not even close to reality.

During any type of disaster or crisis, a leader must overcommunicate with their students, staff, and constituents. Communication brings reassurance, calms nerves, and helps your followers trust you. It makes them more likely to accept your directives and follow you to safety.

STEADFAST CONSISTENCY

The second leadership lesson learned through the pandemic was steadfast consistency. Change always freaks people out. Change during a pandemic really freaks people out. Frequent change during a pandemic sends people overboard.

Some change is necessary and mandated, such as the initial complete school closures and mandated distance learning for all. However, some change is optional. Administrators are given a choice on if and how they will implement changes.

For instance, some school districts in California were given the option of using a school reopening waiver application process that was available for schools in communities with high COVID numbers. Private schools were the first to submit this waiver for reopening. Parents of private school students jumped on this opportunity, saying, "We didn't pay this expensive tuition just for our student to sit at home and be instructed via distance learning. Not even during a pandemic." Whether or not you agree with this line of thinking, the fact is that the vast majority of schools that reopened through the waiver were private schools.

All of a sudden, this waiver opportunity sent local public schools into a tizzy. They were scrambling to keep up. Parents put the pressure on public schools—big time. They asked schools to reopen, even saying, "You are taking away my child's fundamental right to a free and public education." Parents threatened to leave the district. Some actually started disenrolling their students, chasing after the schools that had opened their doors.

Meanwhile, district administrators were not thinking big picture. Leaders very well knew that if only a few students in their school got the virus, it would shut the entire operation down. Yet they became susceptible to the pressure of public opinion and threatening parents. They recognized the lost dollars that would result from losing too many students. Many caved to the pressure to reopen, despite their better judgment.

Schools reopened rapidly, only to quickly close again due to an outbreak. These schools' desire to give in to public opinion led to a knee-jerk reaction, which quickly turned into emotional whiplash for students, staff, and families. No one could ever predict what would happen next. Parents couldn't predict when they would need childcare, when their children would be home, and when they would be at school. The administrators' desire to cave to public desires was actually creating an unpredictable, constantly changing environment for students and staff.

However, thoughtful administrators chose the less popular path. They completely supported the school board's decision to not apply for a reopening waiver, despite several families' complete dismay with the organization. Due to the decision, they lost many families and knew they could potentially lose more. The board was completely aware of the possibility of student attrition.

Instead of rushing to reopen via this waiver, the school board thoughtfully prioritized student and staff health, instructional consistency for students, and minimal risk and liability to the schools. They brought the neediest learners back to campus in very small group cohorts for additional instructional support, but they did not reopen their doors to entire grade levels or grade spans, despite this being a very unpopular approach. They knew that if they reopened, they would likely close again quickly with little warning. At every step, they minimized sudden changes as much as possible.

Thoughtful leaders asked themselves this question: "What would it be like if I contributed to the spread of the virus, which resulted in the illness and even death of one of my staff or family members?" Their caution led to the path of wisdom, which ultimately led to the path of highest consistency for students and family. They tried not to make sudden changes.

The decision not to reopen prematurely was a difficult one for administrators. They experienced depression from the pure heartbreak of not seeing children on campus. Administrators missed the kids. They wanted this crisis to be over. NOW.

However, they knew that if they refused to use common sense and strategic planning, they might as well issue their letter of resignation now. This is to not say reponing schools via the waiver process was a bad decision. Regardless of the route taken, administrators needed to understand how their decisions would impact their staff and families in big ways. A school superintendent said something profound in his address canceling school: "In the end, it will be impossible to know if we overreacted or did too much, but it will be quite apparent if we underreacted or did too little."

No matter what kind of emergency or crisis you face, ensure you focus on building a steadfast character that your people can depend on. Remain stable and predictable. Build trust during turbulent times.

DON'T LISTEN TO THE HYPE

The heat was on from parents, and it included a lot of unnecessary hype, fake news, and fabricated fear.

"It is a hoax," they say.

"Children are not susceptible to this virus," they say.

But what do *you* say? You are the leader, and it's your responsibility to thoroughly research issues and make wise decisions for staff and families. It is really easy to make those claims when it is not your responsibility to keep children and their families safe. It is really easy to tell the leadership to disregard the pandemic when you are not the one that will be dealing with the potential devastation of the decision to rush to bring children back. It's easy to say the pandemic is being blown out of proportion because of politics when you are not the one who will have to sit with your guilt if a student or staff member dies of the virus.

Even without knowing the course of this pandemic and where the world was headed, administrators did their best. All they could do was wait. They had to remain committed to offering staff and families the steadfast consistency they so desperately needed. They had to listen to their own wisdom, intuition, and the advice of wise counselors. They had to ignore the chatter around them and remain on the path they believed was best.

You will never be able to make everyone happy. As discussed in an earlier chapter, haters are always gonna hate. You are serving families with a range of opinions, and there's no way to please everyone at the same time. Let go of people pleasing as you seek to make fast-paced, emotionally charged decisions with a clear head. Decide what is best for your community and act on it.

The principles learned during the 2020 pandemic are true for any local or worldwide crisis. Keep your head on straight, do your best, and protect the people in your care.

FOLLOW LOCAL AND NATIONAL GUIDELINES

Sometimes the government makes it easy for you by creating mandates that you are obliged to follow. These state mandates and health orders are not an option, despite the political pressure from your community. Take a deep breath and remain committed to following the guidelines.

It's also important to communicate the exact essential language of the mandates to the school community. New requirements are ever-changing. Make sure your descriptions, rules, and guidelines are stated as explicitly as possible. Leave no room for misinterpretation.

Understand the fine line between communicating your personal political viewpoints and the state mandates. Most of the time, personal politics need to be left out of the conversation. At the same time, your point of view will often come through, however subtly, in the messages you send. Be aware of how you are coming across. Work to be inclusive of the wide range of opinions of the families in your care.

No matter the disaster you are facing, do your best to work with law enforcement, detectives, emergency response crews, and relief organizations. Network with others to provide an unwavering front of protection to the people you serve.

FOCUS ON MENTAL HEALTH

The pandemic put the entire educational system under almost unbearable stress. Teachers went through the wringer. They had to learn new web-hosting programs. They were forced to transition to online learning before they felt ready. They had to struggle with keeping children engaged from the other end of the screen.

Some felt depressed while teaching to an empty screen full of turned-off videos. There was no way to know if the children on the other end were even awake—or even in the room. Furthermore, teachers felt worried about the learning losses that were occurring. While working from home, they deeply missed the everyday support and camaraderie from fellow teachers.

At the same time, parents struggled with the constant stress of never knowing when kids would be sent into distance education. Some had to stay home from work to babysit their distance learners. Others felt forced to leave their children home alone all day, worrying about the children's safety and their ability to keep themselves on task.

Students also took the brunt of online learning. Kids missed their friends, teachers, and the structure that school provided. Many children felt scared, depressed, and alone. For sufferers of domestic abuse, there were no schoolteachers to notice the bruises. Children could turn off the camera and no one would ever know what was really going on at home. Some teens and kids began attempting suicide at alarming rates.

Many school districts began focusing on intentional mental health interventions for online learners. Teachers were given special suicide risk protocols for distance learning situations. Kids learned deep breathing, stress response habits, and ways to calm themselves.

During any time of crisis, it's important to focus on the mental health of the student, parents, and staff in your care. Whether a shooting, an earthquake, or another type of loss, your students and staff will need grief counseling, mental health support, and possibly financial or physical aid. Don't get so focused on being the "bad guy" and sticking up for what is right that you forget to also be the good guy who provides the help and healing where it is most desperately needed.

And don't neglect your own mental health. Be gentle with yourself. It's impossible to be everything to everyone at all times. Sometimes, you will need to realize that this situation is truly beyond your control. There are things you simply cannot do. You are not superman, and you can't save the entire world at one time. At the end of the day, if you have done all you could, you must allow yourself to detach, disconnect, and rest.

THE TRUE NORTH

A crisis is a time of high stakes, and it demands high discipline from a superintendent or administrator. Ultimately, you do not deserve to be a superintendent during a crisis if you are going to give in to the pressures of the cool kids' club just to achieve instant gratification. You do not deserve to be a leader during this time if you are not willing to take the hits from people who disagree with you. And most of all, you do not deserve to be an administrator right now if you are not willing to take the road less traveled instead of blindly following the masses.

Protect your organization. This means you gear up for battle. You are going to take the hits often if not every day. The stress is going to affect you in huge ways. Work-life balance will cease to exist.

But through it all, protect your organization with your entire being. Stand up to the outside pressures that push you to rush through the process. Do not ever forget about the precious faces that are depending on YOU to keep them safe. Do not ever forget about the people you must take care of. You are a leader, not just an instructional leader. You are here to stand up for your organization, which means *protecting your people.* All of them.

Chapter 8

Progress Is Progress

Keeping Your Focus on the Right Goals

High Accountability. Test Scores. Data Analysis.

Feeling a little queasy yet? Sometimes, your head can start to spin as you look at all the numbers. The students' test scores aren't as high as you'd hoped. The learning objectives aren't always met. You think perhaps they need better computers, better reading intervention programs, and a few more instructional support staff. But at the same time, parents are hankering after a new playground. And you yourself had really been hoping for a new paint job and even some nice outdoor seating where you could sit outside and eat lunch on a nice day.

As a leader, you understand the importance of continuous improvement, and it's up to you to discover which technology purchases, reading initiatives, and new ideas will provide measurable solutions to the problems. You must sift through endless opportunities, evaluate staff requests, and consider parent demands. You try to find the curriculum that will improve student performance while staying within your budget and matching the current capacity of your staff.

All these tasks can feel overwhelming. Sometimes, you may feel like you're wading through endless opportunities. You're unsure which direction to turn, and you need some concrete guideposts to direct you on the journey towards constant growth and improvement. Here are some important things to remember.

KNOW YOUR GOAL

With so many options in front of you, it's critical to know where you're headed. When you haphazardly throw money at various needs and demands, you realize that you never really make much progress. Instead, it's important to develop a strategic plan. Every decision you make should fit into that over-arching, long-term direction for the district.

Simon Sinek, author of *Start with Why,* emphasized the importance of defining not only your path, but also your purpose. He says, "Very few people or companies can clearly articulate WHY they do WHAT they do. By WHY I mean your purpose, cause or belief—WHY does your company exist? WHY do you get out of bed every morning? And WHY should anyone care? People don't buy WHAT you do, they buy WHY you do it."[1]

Developing a strategic plan is a smart way to ensure leaders in the district stay focused on goals and actions. They must have a reason to make deci-sions, a vision that will help them keep moving forward with purpose and direction. The strategic plan should outline the district's mission and vision statements, core values, goals, and the daily and quarterly actions that will lead to fulfilling those goals. Here are some practical tools you can use to develop your own strategic plan.

MISSION AND VISION

First, you must start with identifying the mission and vision of your organiza-tion. This could be the vision of an individual school or an entire district. Ask yourself what is truly most important to your organization. When push comes to shove, what do you want teachers and staff to prioritize?

After you've identified the key priorities, these values need to be put into writing. Rehearse them regularly so that teachers, staff, community members, and students are familiar with them. When repeated frequently, these values and mission statements will begin to guide the daily actions and behaviors of your staff and students.

FLESH OUT THE VISION IN PRACTICAL STEPS

Next, you must define measurable ways in which you plan to pursue your mission and vision while adhering to your core values. You'll identify your most important priorities. You'll identify some key goals, and then you'll define an action plan for each year. The action plan will be broken down into smaller goals with strategies, tactics, and metrics that will help you know when you've been successful.

DIFFERENT VISIONS AND DIFFERENT OUTCOMES

Although it may seem that putting words on paper won't make a measurable impact on the district, this couldn't be farther from the truth. As a practical example, let's examine the mission statements of several schools and districts around the country. We'll see how these differing visions ultimately affect the direction the district heads.

One district in the Midwest has a stated mission to "prepare all students to achieve college, career and life readiness through an innovative and rigorous educational experience." Their vision is to "be the district of choice in our region, where all students and staff are empowered to dream, believe and achieve." Their values include "student success, safety and belonging, family and community collaboration, visionary leadership, civic engagement, and equity and diversity."[2]

The Midwestern school district fleshes out their plan in several measurable steps. They hope to increase graduation rate and third-grade reading proficiency through increasing the use of Writing, Inquiry, Collaboration, Organization, and Reading (WICOR); increasing certifications and college credit by utilizing career pathways; and making schools a trusted, safe place by working to create safe "physical spaces."[3]

One of the district's top stated priorities is becoming the district of choice. As a result, staff shape their decisions around making sure they don't lose students. They focus on the per-capita government funding they want to receive. They work overtime to enroll students at the prekindergarten level and to attract new students from surrounding areas. Decisions during COVID are focused not only on safety (another of their key goals) but also on ensuring they do not lose students to surrounding private schools. In other words, goals inform daily actions.

Let's look at another example of how a mission informs daily actions. This California Charter School Management organization has a mission to "provide a rich, meaningful education in a nurturing environment, where students are continually challenged and their natural curiosity, creativity, and talents can thrive."[4] They state that their goal is to help students become "virtuous, courageous, and intelligent citizens, equipped with a love of learning and a love of life."[5] They also hope to develop "grit, tenacity, and empathy" in students.[6]

The charter school also has strong values. This school hopes to "promote individual strengths and respond to individual needs in order to nurture growth, self-confidence, courage, and resilience." They want to "respect each other's differences and learn in cooperation with one another." They want their students to "develop their interests and impact positive change," and to "challenge each other to think critically and creatively to explore, problem solve, and encourage new ideas."[7] Most of all, they hope students will "engage by connecting their interests and learning to develop awareness of self, community, and world."[8]

Practically, these goals are fleshed out in day-to-day steps. The charter school is planning to implement restorative practices, a system of positive behavior management. But it's not just planning to blast its teachers with one training and expect them to implement it from there. Instead, they plan to specifically create practical tools like "flow charts," "routines and transition techniques," and a "playbook for highly accountable centers-based work."[9]

They know where they are headed, and they know the steps needed to get there. They will hire outside training and support coaches to help the teachers learn the nitty-gritty of this approach. They will provide time for staff to collaborate on learning.

The charter school organization has multiple stated goals, and it has specific plans about how they will work towards each specific goal in measurable ways.

- There will be additional training provided to staff in areas of reading intervention, discipline practices, and more.
- They will hire staff that can help with behaviorally challenged children.
- They'll provide after-school programs and homework support, along with clubs to help students grow in their interests.
- They'll give students practical opportunities to self-assess and reflect on their own growth and achievements.
- They'll provide classes that help parents learn healthy ways of relating to their kids.

In short, none of their goals are vague and directionless. Each goal has practical steps that will be taken, year by year, by specific people at specific times in the district.

How do the priorities of this charter school organization compare to the goals of the first district examined earlier? How does a change in focus change the outcome? The charter school is focusing on the process (grit, empathy, curiosity, and love of learning), while the former district is focusing on the product (being the district of choice or creating high school graduates).

How does this impact the daily actions of students, parents, and teachers? When teachers and students focus on curiosity and love of learning (process), the kids will automatically want to keep learning and graduate from high school (product). And as students' interests are cultivated and they grow in self-awareness, courage, and empathy (process), parents will automatically gravitate towards this district as a wonderful environment for their child to grow (product). But focusing only on the product without clear steps for the process leads to ambiguity.

When you create your goals, ensure that they are measurable, achievable, and practical. Keep goals to no more than five, in order to narrow the focus to the most important priorities. Then thoroughly acquaint your staff and families with these goals until they know them by heart.

Now that you have a purpose, vision, and goals, you'll have an easier time making decisions about continuous improvement. When in doubt, consult your five-year plan. Decide whether this purchase fits into your overarching goals.

FOCUS ON PERSONALIZED STUDENT ENGAGEMENT

Have you ever reviewed student data with a sinking feeling? As you scanned each test score and scrolled through the data analysis, did you ever feel that something was missing? Deep down, did you realize that all those statistics, key targets, and number data didn't reflect a deep, profound reality?

Are you tired of the constant graphs and spreadsheets that tell you very little about each child as a learner? Sure, a number on a paper will indicate growth or a lack of in a particular area, but it by no means tells the entire picture of each student. Do you think it's time to find something new?

Perhaps you realize that none of the statistics can reflect the true learning that is going on in the classroom. You understand that pressuring children and teachers to perform for tests isn't always the best path towards integrated higher thinking skills. And there are many priceless moments that happen in the classroom that never show up on tests.

None of those numbers or statistics can reflect the delight of a personalized unit study one of your most creative teachers did with her students last quarter. The hard data doesn't show the strategizing, teamwork, creativity, and research the kids did. It doesn't demonstrate the way the learning ignited the students' dreams for the future. It doesn't show the light-bulb moments, one-on-one conversations about mental health, or any of the other impromptu learning opportunities that contribute towards deep, integrated, successful learning.

Yes, data analysis and test scores are important, and each is part of a successful leadership plan. But if the numbers aren't reflecting what you or your superiors had hoped for, it's important to stop and breathe. You know that there is more to education than charts and graphs. If continuous improvement is the goal, this is exactly what your focus should be—not on numbers.

One of the most important values that all administrators should keep at the forefront is personalized, engaging student learning. Even though you know this fact cognitively, it's easy to become caught in the spell of obsessing over test score improvement, graduation rates, truancy, and all those other things that are a part of your accountability system. After all, if your school meets those goals, then doesn't that mean you are an amazing leader? It's easy to go this route, but you must consider a few other factors that are also at play.

Over the past few years, it has become increasingly clear that when good teaching and high student interest is the focus, the rest takes care of itself. Schools focused on the right areas have blazed a trail and shown what successful teaching looks like. They emphasize each learner's absolute potential rather than arbitrary test results.

Sure, every learner must still take the annual standardized tests. Those scores are most definitely reflected on the school's yearly report card to parents. The difference, though, is what happens every other day that the student is not testing. Teachers really get to know their learners so they can tap into their interests. Then they give the students latitude and choice to pursue the learning style and content that piques the child's unique creativity.

This learning environment provides a win-win for everyone. Behavior issues are kept at a minimum, and students are excited (most of the time) about their part in the learning. Teachers become facilitators of a beautiful process of discovery, rather than being only the deliverers of content.

The beauty of individualized, interest-based learning is that it recognizes the different learning styles, needs, and quirks of each individual student. Teachers and administrators must understand that the spectrum of children's preferred learning methods is very different. Let's consider four very different learners.

1. Bryce gets it all done quickly, rushing to check off all the boxes. Political debates, sports, guitar class, and jazz band are what really light his fire.
2. Aria takes her time doing a meticulous job. She is her own worst critic and obsessive about routines and organization. Her hobby is cheerleading.
3. Jaden talks way too much in class, wanting to be the first to answer questions. He gets bored easily if he isn't actively learning something of interest. He is a basketball fanatic and school is "just okay" to him.
4. Jane is easily distracted and needs a lot of external motivation to focus. But when she kicks it in gear, there is nothing that stops her. She is highly creative, perfecting her baking and art skills most days.

Let's suppose all four learners are the same age and in the same class. One child needs a quiet environment with plenty of individual encouragement. Another needs active, exciting debates and challenges. One thrives on conversation and interaction, while another needs plenty of work and space to complete tasks on her own. Each one has his or her own individual social needs, learning challenges, and interests.

This is the exact reality of the classroom, except most teachers must factor in the challenges and needs of 20–40 additional students, as well. Teachers are faced with a challenge, and it's not ideal to cookie-cutter the method of instruction for all of these learners.

Instead, teachers on the front lines must form relationships, getting to know the children, and use so many different tools and approaches to keep each of them engaged. They must understand that each child has very unique personalities and needs. This is just one of the reasons why teachers are miracle workers.

Yet administrators wonder why teachers become frustrated when they see their administrators hyperfocus on test scores and all the data that goes along with it. As administrators, it is worthwhile to take a step back and realize that there's more to learning than test scores.

GOOD TEACHERS ARE KEY

Teachers are truly the key to the success of an individualized learning program. There is not one publisher's curriculum that can truly tap into each of these learning styles and replace really good teaching. Sure, content is presented better in some curriculum than others. But no curriculum by itself can engage students at the high level needed to truly draw students to the task at hand. Creative, engaged teachers provide the imagination, care, and creativity that students need to succeed.

Allow teachers wide latitude in teaching the content. Imagine the potential for growth that could happen when a teacher takes a content standard or skill and thinks, "The sky's the limit!" This teacher is free to allow the students to show their knowledge in creative ways. Kids can be artistic, they can be presenters, they can be collaborators, they can be innovators. This critical, solid foundational teaching prepares students to become readers, writers, and mathematicians that excel in many areas of their lives.

UTILIZE CURRICULUM AND UNIT STUDIES

Allow teachers to use project-based learning units that pique the interest of their students. For example, a class of first and second grade teams in a California school recently enjoyed a unit on "Heroes." Teachers prompted students with essential questions, such as, "What makes a person a hero?"

No, this is not a Common Core standard in first or second grade. But you better bet that through this highly interesting topic, the students were reading, writing, and presenting about an influential hero of their choice. They were citing textual evidence at a very young age, which is very much an essential standard.

Not only did these young learners conduct their own research, but they also had the chance to creatively share what they learned. Their culminating activity was dressing up as the hero of their choice to present to their scholar colleagues. Students chose heroes such as Jacques Cousteau, Ruth Bader Ginsburg, and Abraham Lincoln. Through these learning opportunities, children truly integrated their learning into all aspects of their educational journey.

PROVIDE EXTRACURRICULAR OPTIONS

Clubs and after-school activities provide an opportunity for children to explore their interests in a less-pressured, less academic setting. When students are given multiple extra and co-curricular options to choose from, they establish a real connection to the school.

However, districts often cut visual and performing arts options due to lack of money. This choice is disheartening. Removing this opportunity is an outright disservice to this nation's future society. Without the opportunity to grow and explore their interests, students' motivation diminishes.

Yes, it's understandable that a reduction in funding is the driving force behind these decisions. But when these opportunities are cut off the top without considering other types of expenditures that will not directly impact the student experience, schools better be ready for an increase in student boredom and behavior problems. It's unrealistic to expect the students, who are at least as distracted as adults, to survive educational experiences that do not truly get to the heart and soul of their interests.

CREATE EARLY CAREER PATHWAYS

A popular trend in high schools is career technical education (CTE). These career pathways focus on a particular topic such as technology, healthcare, and communications, with the purpose of exposing students to a career path in their high school years. Students are allowed to build stage sets, work on cars, build airplanes, and cook with a commercial food-handling license— right in their own school building! Other times, students are bused to a community college to start their career path while still in high school. This is wonderful, and it can be argued that this approach to learning needs to start much earlier than high school.

Student learning outside of the four walls of the classroom can and should happen early on, even during the primary grades. Schools miss the mark when they are hyperfocused only on student progress, meeting proficiency, and state content standards. Instead, administrators should be hyperfocused on preparing their scholars to be contributors to a global society from the get-go.

Practically, how can this be done? Rather than putting all of a school's "eggs" into the "standards mapping" basket, administrators should start asking themselves, "What amazing experiences should we provide our students?"

Some schools were 100% committed to providing exciting learning experiences for their students. They even provided these opportunities during the COVID-19 pandemic. During the shut-down, the school distributed gardening kits to every distance learner, preschool to grade 8. These kits not only provided cool hands-on learning experiences, but also allowed scholars to engage in ongoing learning as they observed the growth of their gardens. As they wrote essays about their observations in the garden, they also performed counting, measuring, and simple math. This provided the opportunity for writing, math, and oral language, hitting many state content standards in a creative and engaging way.

If engaging learning opportunities can be provided during the pandemic, they can certainly be provided at the school building. A school in the Midwest provides daily opportunity for their students to interact with animals. Almost every room of the school has a snake, a butterfly, a lizard, or a rabbit. A therapy dog roams the property with its owners. Bees fly in and out from the glass beehive, allowing students to watch the creation of honey. Outside on the playground, a flock of chickens provides opportunities to learn about eggs and meat production. Children are given the opportunity to use wheelbarrows and other tools to haul supplies. As children care for the animals, they learn about safety, protection from predators, concern for others, and the value of hard work. Every fall, the teachers take their kids camping in the wilderness for several days at a time.

Yet another school decided to plant a garden of native prairie grasses with their students. Children helped put together planters, plant vegetables, and water the native grasses. A Native American came to the school to bless the garden, helping the children understand the culture and history of the prairies.

Other magnet schools focus on technology, aeronautics, art, or music. Children have the opportunity to explore their interests early in life. They gain knowledge and experience in gardening, animal husbandry, technology, and environmental care. These experiences are invaluable for young people.

Progress should not only be perceived as high stakes test success. There is a major flaw with that mindset which results in an even bigger disservice for students. If your focus is only on how the student is doing on the test or the assessment, you will completely lose sight of the amazing experiences students deserve to tap into which will most definitely contribute to their future career paths.

A test does not and should not tell the whole story of the learner. Instead, administrators must look at learners as the unique people they are. They each have unique and beautiful gifts. Teachers and administrators need to take time to find out what their talents and interests are and design learning experiences with those in mind. It is absolutely the school's job to differentiate well and to engage with students.

TAKE SMALL STEPS

While continuous improvement is always the goal, it's important to move forward in a way that doesn't shake your organization with too many new initiatives at once. It's important to evaluate your next steps and determine an overarching plan. Then, move forward in a sustainable way that doesn't overwhelm your teachers or your organization.

For instance, perhaps you enjoyed reading about the school that planted gardens, raised animals, and took their kids camping every year as a school field trip. Further, you've heard good things about restorative justice, which entails a mindset shift around discipline. You went to a training which emphasized the importance of getting kids to read by third grade, and you've decided that a reading initiative is in order. And to top it all off, you read about the learning benefits of the Gomez and Gomez model that pairs students with learning buddies and incorporates a rich vocabulary into every aspect of their learning day. You're excited about the potential of each of these initiatives, and you'd like to see them implemented right away.

At the next meeting, you unload your goals on your staff. You want gardens outside every classroom, one animal per teacher, Restorative Circle Groups, and a completely different structure of discipline that no longer relies on office referrals. You'd like your teachers to implement reading initiatives, vocabulary walls, rich language learning, and learning buddies in classrooms. And of course, they will continue to uphold Rigor, WICOR, and all manner of other initiatives you've already introduced. You're pumped about these opportunities, and you hope your staff shares your vision.

But as you gather up your notes, pass out the handouts, and walk down from the podium, what response do you think you will receive? Your staff will start sending emails. They will snag you in the hall to express their concerns.

Their fears are valid. They are worried that if they ditch office referrals, the entire school will fall apart, since the staff is still untrained and has no idea how to implement the Restorative Justice approach. The teachers complain that they don't know how to do Circle groups, and while they are learning, the kids will get away with all manner of misdemeanors.

Furthermore, they are worrying about time constraints. How can they implement these reading initiatives while the children are also outside setting up a chicken coop? When will they have time to make the vocabulary cards and set up the learning buddies? And where are they going to get the money to take care of the pets?

As you can see, it's simply impossible to make too many changes at one time. Your staff will either mutiny, or they will dutifully try to uphold your initiatives without the support and infrastructure they need to be successful. But in short order, many of the grand ideas you've had will fall by the wayside because there was not a sustainable, slowly built structure that could hold them up.

Instead of moving quickly, choose the initiative that is top priority. Spend time getting to know your staff's thoughts and finding out their concerns about the ideas you are thinking of bringing to the table. Don't push initiatives on staff when they are not ready. Instead, support their needs until they can get on board with the direction you are moving the school or district.

FISCAL RESPONSIBILITY

Attempting to begin many initiatives at one time is unwise from a staffing perspective. But it's also unwise from a financial perspective. Continuous improvement often includes expenditures for new equipment, building updates, and learning tools. But for continuous improvement to take place, the district must continue operating in the green, while still purchasing the things that are needed to improve student learning.

Although you can improve student learning and focus on continuous improvement while operating in the red, you are now creating another big problem for yourself. You can't spend endless money on technology, a new playground, and new creative ventures, all the while ignoring the fact that you are putting the district in financial turmoil.

As a new school administrator, you probably have dozens of ideas of how to improve the district. You want to spend money on new TVs in all the classroom. You want to put in new playground equipment so that the children's brains can be enriched by movement and activity. You have dozens of ideas to improve the looks, aesthetics, and feel of your school or the schools in your district.

In their excitement, new superintendents often lose sight of the financial shape of the district. They're only thinking about the needs of the district.

They have good intent for continuous improvement and grandiose plans about what they want to do to improve the school. They're always moving forward and looking towards the next step. But they have zero understanding of how much money is going out for these initiatives to get them done.

Here are some practical tools that will help you balance your ideas for continuous improvement with the realistic constraints of finances.

ELIMINATE FLUFF

The first step to responsibly handling money is recognizing what is truly important and what is just "fluff." From your first day in office, people will start begging for expenditures. Parents want new tables and umbrellas for outdoor seating. The janitors ask for a new marquis and signage out on the front of the school. You, the new administrator, hope that the new marquis you buy will also light up at night.

You want all these things. But are they actually the things that contribute to student learning? Curb appeal is nice. You want the school to look good. You wish for state-of-the-art equipment. You need to consider if these expenditures are aligned to your district's goals.

Leaders should always be prioritizing first the expenditure on student learning. If the kids don't have solid curriculum and books, and necessary instructional materials, then none of that other stuff matters.

Believe it or not, field trips can also fall into the "fluff" category. Spending too much money on field trips is an expenditure trap that's easy to fall into. After all, you reason, these field trips are directly improving the children's learning. They're providing personal experiences and out-of-the-classroom adventures. Isn't that what education is all about?

Yes, field trips are great. In fact, they're wonderful. But they're also very expensive. As an administrator, you need to work with teachers and donors to provide ways for students to have experiences outside the four walls of the classroom—without breaking the budget. Perhaps you can go to a nearby museum instead of taking the students in a bus to an expensive amusement park eight hours away. Find ways you can tone down the field trips while still providing the students with exciting experiences, such as bringing guest speakers into the classroom.

Spend time carefully prioritizing the relative importance of your spending items. Student learning is first, and other less important cosmetic improvements will come later.

FIND OTHER FUNDING SOURCES

At times, you will need to prioritize a seemingly less important funding item. You can't afford it with school money, and it's not crucial for student success. But it's still important to implement this improvement sooner, rather than later. When this happens, you'll need to find additional funding sources that are willing to help you achieve your short-term goal.

Let's say there's an elementary school with a desperate lack of shade in the playground. The parents are saying, "You know what? You guys have hardly any shade out there. It gets blazing hot in the summer, 110 degrees. Kids go out to recess, both before school and after school, and there's no shade to stand under during 30-minute periods. They're hot. It's unsafe. They overheat. They're running around. Why can't you build a shade structure?"

As you review plans and estimates, you realize a shade structure is going to cost your school $100,000 dollars. You ask yourself, "Can we afford a shade structure? Is the shade structure a priority over other demands?"

There are many other expenditures which have been requested by parents and teachers. Is the shade structure more important than new computers for the classrooms? You recognize that you don't have an endless amount of funds, and you have to prioritize which expenditure is the most important, while not operating in the red.

At first, you hope you can compromise, buying a little of this and a little of that to make everyone happy. But it's hard to successfully make everyone happy this way. It's a rare feat. You can't build only half of a shade structure.

Finally, you decide that it's more important for your students to all have Chromebooks than it is for the shade. You communicate this message back to parents. But you also provide your back-up plan.

You explain, "We will prioritize funding the shade structure during next year."

Or you say, "We have a long-term plan to implement the shade structure in the next five years."

Possibly, you find other options for building the shade structure this year. One of the most creative back-up strategies you can pull out of your hat is to find other sources of funding. When you realize that a certain expenditure is not a high priority academically, but it is important socially, you can ask for help from other places.

Many schools have a strong PTO (Parent Teacher Organization) that can hold fundraisers to raise money for needed expenditures. After all, if it's the parents who are hankering after a shade structure, leave it to the parents to motivate their fellow moms and dads to donate to the cause. PTO funding structures can be of great assistance for these side issues. Maybe they can't fund the whole thing, but they can cover some of it.

In addition, there are many other service clubs that offer donations to schools. The Rotary Club, the Kiwanis, and the Lions are just a few options to look at. Many of them are eager to help out as a source of funding.

GET INPUT

As a leader, you need to get feedback from others rather than making decisions all by yourself. Get input about what the district needs, directly from the stakeholders. Financial decisions should not be all about you as the leader. You shouldn't just throw your weight around, saying, "I want this and that."

Instead, you as a site leader or district leader need to receive feedback from the board, from staff, and from parents. Each of these groups will give you insights on necessary expenditures. Only then can you carefully balance and prioritize the relative importance of each financial need. Demonstrate to your constituents that you care about their needs.

Furthermore, it's your job to know the budget so well that you can easily determine what you can afford and what you can't. Like a household budget, you must know what's coming in and what's going out. You always prioritize not spending more than what's coming in.

The chief business officer or business manager is your best friend when it comes to understanding how your fund expenditures align with your continuous improvement plan. Your business officer can alert you to factors you would never notice otherwise. They can point out information about energy usage in school buildings, alternate energy sources, and how to conserve. They will assist you in "managing the physical assets of the district" and help you prioritize expenditures for a sustainable future.[10] The business manager can help you keep track of when the buildings were last painted and updated, and at what time these upkeep needs become urgent rather than "fluff." Furthermore, the chief business officer can help "prepare preliminary cost estimates, develop a prioritization process, and identify funding sources."[11]

Don't try to go it alone. Rely on the experts who can help you understand the financial side of administration.

REDEFINE PROGRESS

Don't be discouraged if you can't afford every new goal that you'd like to pursue. Continuous improvement is always the goal, but money often stands in the way. This is not your fault, and it doesn't mean you're not moving forward. Instead, you may need to redefine what progress and improvement looks like in your district.

Achieving fiscal responsibility, *in and of itself*, is progress. Never forget that staying in the green is an accomplishment. For one thing, it means you get to keep your job and continue to impact students. Financial irresponsibility equals career suicide; inability to handle a budget constitutes the top reason superintendents leave their job. Irresponsible spending and operating in the red can mean an end to your job. So when you achieve financial security for the district, you *are* continually improving—even if you can't afford the new initiative you had hoped for.

In addition, keep in mind other kinds of progress that are harder to quantify. For example, no statistic can truly measure the glow on a student's face when he finally understands phonics in fourth grade. He's years behind his peers, but after years of patient and tireless work with his one-on-one tutor, he's finally had a breakthrough. Test scores still place him in the lowest percentile, but his personal achievement is priceless. You realize you have to find a way to honor that and provide him with an exciting and motivating learning experience—even if test scores never reflect this.

Redefine progress, and you'll begin to see it all around you. When you reframe everyday small successes, you'll realize that you are making progress, slowly but surely.

THE TRUE NORTH

Progress should not only be perceived as high stakes test success. Neither is it measured only in terms of new and improved cosmetics. It is not defined by purchasing the absolute newest technology devices.

Instead, continuous improvement stays true to your stated purposes, focuses on student learning, and is financially responsible. As a leader, you must remember that you have been charged with gearing up the future generation of leaders. This must take place in many differentiated ways that include your long-term goals.

Do you truly believe you are contributing to this type of culture in your own district? Would you want to be a student in your classrooms? Does the learning engage you? Answering yes means that you are well on your way to giving your students the incredible education they deserve.

NOTES

1. Simon Sinek, *Start with Why: How Great Leaders Inspire Everyone to Take Action* (New York City: Portfolio, 2011), as quoted in Sam T. Davis, "Start with Why by Simon Sinek," accessed December 2, 2021, https://www.samuelthomasdavies.com/book-summaries/business/start-with-why/.

2. "Every Student Future Ready: The WPS Strategic Plan 2018–2023," Accessed November 9, 2021, https://www.usd259.org/cms/lib/KS01906405/Centricity/Domain/4393/StratPlan-Year4-Spreads.pdf.

3. Ibid.

4. The Academies Charter Management Organization 2019–2024 Strategic Plan, 3.

5. Ibid., 3.

6. Ibid., 3.

7. Ibid., 4.

8. Ibid., 5.

9. Ibid., 8.

10. "21st Century Schools and the Role of the CBO," *Casbo 2014 Annual Conference,* Accessed December 2, 2021, https://dcgstrategies.com/wp-content/uploads/2015/07/Workshop-Supplement-CASBO-2014-21st-Century-Schools.pdf.

11. Ibid.

Chapter 9

Branding

Public Perception Is Everything

Facebook. Insta. Twitter. LinkedIn. Does social media excite you? Does it terrify you? It's common to hear superintendents remark that social media is just "too dangerous." Afraid of the negative fallout, these leaders choose to never post online. Some have even cancelled their social media accounts.

It's understandable to have concerns about time wastage, internet privacy, and piracy when using online means of communication. However, these concerns shouldn't keep you from leveraging the powerful tool of social media. Without it, you miss out on an important opportunity to present yourself and your school winsomely and accurately to the wider community.

Social media can in fact be your number one success tool when used strategically. Successful social media use all boils down to one element: branding. Branding is the ability to present a consistent narrative about yourself, your school, and your district to the watching world. Branding is an important aspect of leadership—one that admin preparation classes often fail to address.

In the next pages, you will learn some powerful aspects of branding, publicity, and social media that are important to understand as a leader.

MANAGING PERCEPTIONS

Anyone with a background in advertising will tell you that the public perceptions created through branding can make or break you professionally. Perception is everything. Creating a powerful positive narrative about your school's identity can attract positive attention and stimulate internal growth. On the other hand, a lack of communication or a negative presentation can plummet you and your organization into disaster.

Some may object, "Does it matter what other people think of us? Should we even care?" The short answer is, "Yes." Have you ever had an employee who boasts, "I do not care what people think of me"? You probably realized in short order that this staff member was a liability and a nightmare. They likely left a trail of carelessness behind them, not worrying about their effect on others. They were not self-aware and unable to monitor the way they were coming across to those whose paths they cross. Ultimately, you did not want them working for your organization.

On the other hand, employees who have a healthy respect for others' perceptions will earn your deep respect. They aren't obsessed with people-pleasing, but they're aware of the fact that their actions impact other people around them. In the same way, it's important to use branding to curate the perceptions of others.

TUNE THEIR FOCUS

It's important to be intentional about the messages you are sending to your community. Remember, perception often creates reality. The things that you highlight with your branding will actually start changing the reality of your parents, students, and community.

How can that be? The answer is the Reticular Activating System. A person's mind, brain, and senses are always at work, filtering out sensory input that is not deemed important. But when you realize the importance of a certain aspect of reality, our brains stop filtering that out. They start focusing on it instead.

For example, when someone calls to your attention lightning rods, you suddenly start seeing lightning rods you'd never noticed before. When you start shopping for a car, you suddenly start noticing all the varieties of cars on the highway. When people start to focus on the things they need for success, they start noticing the ingredients for success everywhere they go.[1] You never notice a certain aspect of reality until someone calls it to your attention. Then you see it everywhere.

In the same way, when your branding highlights the positive aspects of the district, your community will start focusing on those aspects. As you constantly bring out the goals and values of your school, your parents will start noticing those elements at play in the district. Instead of seeing only the negative, they start focusing on the positive. What people focus on will guide their way, and you want to guide the thought patterns of your parents and community members in a positive direction.

If you don't define your school to the world, others will do it for you. Parents will start to talk:

"My kid isn't getting the help she needs."

"Let me tell you about my child's experience in seventh grade. That math teacher is no good."

"Can you believe they disciplined the teacher's aide for helping my daughter to read in 3rd grade!?! She was making progress until they took away the para."

"Have you heard about the fights that are going on at the high school?"

Soon, the parents' narratives and experiences start defining the story of the school or the district. The more they focus on these realities, the more they will start noticing the downfalls of the district. Soon, this becomes the dominant story that constantly self-reinforces itself. As a result, the narrative lowers morale and diminishes parent engagement.

When there is no information going out from your district, it's just as bad as distasteful information going out. When there is a lack of powerful, positive branding from the superintendent or principal, parents will move in with narratives to fill the vacuum. When the community isn't receiving communication, or there's not frequent marketing material that is being highlighted and shown, then the community starts to form their own false reality. They create their own perceptions because they don't have the information to form a solid, accurate, truthful story.

As a leader, you need to make sure that you are controlling the narrative. You must write the story of your district and your schools before the community writes the story for you. If you allow others to write your narrative, that story may be something you don't want to read.

Let's look at some practical ways to use branding to powerfully affect what others think about the future of your district.

FOLLOW GOOD EXAMPLES

Social media can be a powerful way to influence your district's perception of you, your leadership, your school, and your goals. When it comes to branding and public perception, you can learn a lot from other influencers and leaders. Turn on your social media apps and start following a multitude of groups and organizations, lawmakers, and other leaders on social media. They are most likely using this powerful tool to express their initiatives and opinions. Watching how they do it will serve as invaluable knowledge to you as a school or district leader. Learn all you can as you educate yourself on their mindset and practical approaches.

Study how other leaders do social media. What personal details do they share? What information do they reserve for their private life? How do color, style, thematic arrangement, and visual appeal play into their brand? What concepts come up repeatedly? What defines the way they present themselves to the world? What can you learn from them?

Furthermore, study how other schools or districts present themselves publicly. What elements of their social media feeds catch your interest? How do they make their school's unique characteristics stand out? How do they brand themselves? What does their social media say about their values, beliefs, and activities?

BRANDING YOUR SCHOOL OR DISTRICT

After studying other examples, it's time to define your school's brand. What do you want your school to be known for? Are you known for student performance, parent involvement, high-quality gifted education, or your trauma-informed restorative justice program? Your five-year plan, mission, vision, and goals should provide key insights into the way you will want to present your brand.

Any time you send out publications, whether through social media, email, or through hard copy snail mail, you are constantly creating narratives about what is happening in the district or the school. Whether you are conscious of it or not, you are forming your brand. Every message you send out affects the way people see your school.

Your goal is to be intentional about the way you present yourself. Remember that you are advertising your school or district, just like a fast-food restaurant or clothing store advertises their products. Keep in mind that you are developing ads for your product. Just like a shoe designer, you are appealing to customers: students, family, community. You have a responsibility to put out tasteful, classy marketing in your public relations campaign.

Here are a few ways you can improve your brand and marketing strategy.

- Create a Consistent Visual Identity. Logos, colors, themes, and images contribute to the way the district is perceived. You want to create a visually pleasing brand that draws people to your organization. After you create a strong visual brand, publish guidelines that help your individual schools stay true to your brand. You can create a written guide that helps district representatives portray a consistent representation of your brand. You may want to designate the way your logo must be presented, the amount of white space that must be around it, the size and spacing in which it should be formatted, the exact colors which should contribute to it, and the fonts that should be included.[2] Make sure that your district is represented consistently and positively.

- Use Video Media. Videos can be a powerful way to engage with your audience. For example, a district in the Midwest has a "Strategic Plan Van" that goes around the district video recording the ways that the schools are contributing to the strategic plan. The superintendent herself drives the van and describes what she sees, raising excitement in the community. In the videos, she interviews students who are doing college and career readiness projects, such as building a real airplane, working on drones, or learning about unique pathways. Videos bring these concepts to life, constantly highlighting the ways that the district is implementing areas of the strategic plan.[3] In addition, other videos on the district's channel celebrate individual teachers, highlight the small ways that teachers are bringing everyday engagement to their classrooms, or even show the principal reading aloud to students.[4] Each one of these videos sends a message that shapes the way that people think about the district.
- Use Physical Signs and Letterheads. For community members who are not active on social media, physical signs can be an excellent way to influence the way the public thinks about the district. Consider creating colorful signs that advertise the goals and strategic plans of the district. Hang them on playground fences and in public places. Make your district's distinctive signs visible to the community.
- Utilize Flyers. Printed newsletters, brochures, and flyers can help you advertise what the school is offering right now. An individual school can use brochures to advertise news about the unit studies, grade level activities, and learning successes. A district can use printed media to highlight the ways that the district is fulfilling its strategic plan. Emphasize interesting events, band concerts, choir programs, and other happenings around the district. Continue to underline the district's mission and vision every chance you get.
- Be Distinctive. What does your district have to offer that the next one does not? What makes your district stand out from the hundreds of other options in the country? Why should someone choose your school or community over the next one? Get creative. The Kankakee School District 111 seamlessly intertwines their school district number with their mission and vision: "One community, One district, One vision, for all children."[5] The Castleberry School District in Texas focuses on high-quality libraries, books, and services, while the Kent School District focuses on gratitude to their community.[6] Mooresville Schools in Indiana focus on their history, while Fall Creek Schools in Wisconsin bases their brand on the familial bonds in their district.[7] Each district emphasizes the unique qualities that make them special.

- Parent Forums. How can parent forums contribute to your brand? Each opportunity to connect to your community is an important ingredient that helps ensure that your district is perceived in a positive light. One district affirms, "A brand is more than the visual identity of an organization. It is our staff, our teachers, our students, our parents. It is the work we do in and with the community. It is the stories we tell about our successes and how we address our challenges. It is every interaction with everyone and everything related to the district. No single person can build up a brand on their own, but every single person can contribute."[8] When the leader holds consistent parent forums, the parents have the opportunity to come hear organization updates. In addition, the parents will have chances to interact with the district about their goals and get their questions answered. That is an example of the leader writing the story of the district. The leader is saying, "This is what's happening. This is what you have to look forward to."

Branding is not just about advertising your school. It's about making sure that people know the awesome things that are going on inside the four walls of your building. Joseph Sanfelippo, speaking of his book *The Power of Branding,* says, "The issue is the stories about schools are being told by people who have no affiliation with schools. The idea of branding schools isn't about selling kids or making false promises . . . it's about promoting the amazing things happening for those not experiencing them on a daily basis. Telling the story of schools helps create a narrative that builds culture and gives everyone in your community an identity."[9] How will you tell your school's story today?

PERSONAL COMMUNICATION

As we've seen, the leader utilizes social media, Instagram, Twitter, and other media to create a narrative in the public mind. This is accomplished not only through branding, but also through personal communication.

In addition to being a powerful branding tool, social media can also be a wonderful tool to bridge the gap and create a more personal connection and communication. Effective communication will reflect back on your branding, helping you continue to create a narrative. Here are some tips to leverage the tool of communication with your students, staff, and parents.

Be Practical

Communication means reaching out to staff and parents in a practical, accessible way. Do your parents ever check their physical mailboxes? If not, then a paper flyer is not the best way to reach them. Similarly, if they don't use email frequently, then stop sending emails. Access them in the ways they're most familiar with. Frequently, this will include texting and social media. Like it or not, Twitter and Instagram are the places where your parents are hanging out. It is incredibly important that leaders use the same media tools that school families are frequently visiting. Families need to be able to relate to their leaders at a very human level.

It can be problematic when no information is going out to the parents through these social media channels. You may be sending out emails, but if your parents aren't getting them, it makes absolutely no difference. When zero information is coming out, people create their own story. Social media is a method of communication that you can use to stay in front of the message. Ensure you're controlling the narrative so your families are not left in the dark and controlling the narrative for you.

Be Purposeful

Communication does not just include informing people about the school's events. Yes, keeping parents up to date with the school's activities and upcoming learning opportunities is a very important element of communication. But most importantly, it's about sharing the purpose of your organization.

You've worked hard to create your mission, your vision, and your values. So now, make those values a prominent part of your communication with parents, staff, and community members. Ensure they know not only *what* you're doing, but *why* you're doing it. Simon Sinek says, "We are drawn to leaders and organizations that are good at communicating what they believe. Their ability to make us feel like we belong, to make us feel special, safe and not alone is part of what gives them the ability to inspire us."[10] Ensure that your communication fosters a sense of belonging and shared purpose in those who read it.

Be Personal

In addition to sharing practical information and purposeful vision, you should also prioritize sharing your personal life with your school, staff, and district. Your kids may be annoyed with the amount of Insta stories you post (especially of them), but this is one important way you can stay connected with your local community.

As you share your life through social media, you will gain a familiarity and camaraderie with those you serve. As you walk on a campus, a parent greets you and says, "Hey! I saw that you were at Shaver Lake over the weekend. How was it?" This simple post can open up a natural, authentic, and easy conversation that will help you connect to and relate with the families that you serve. Or the staff member will meet you on a busy Monday morning and say, "I saw that you were doing the Rotary fundraiser last weekend. How can I help out?" Enough said.

EXERCISING CAUTION WITH SOCIAL MEDIA

Social media can be a powerful tool, but it can also be the number one way to get yourself in a whole lot of trouble. When you post carelessly, you can irreversibly affect the public's perception in a negative way. Once the information is out there, it can never be retracted. So think carefully before you post.

Any leader is just one social media post away from career suicide. The death of one's job can result because of the nature of one's post. This may seem extreme, but be assured that it happens. When a leader is tagged in a Facebook post taking shots of tequila at a friend's birthday on Sunday, they will likely face stiff consequences when showing up to work on Monday. What they did was innocent to some, but highly questionable to many others.

Here is a key insight to keep in mind when you are considering the boundaries of social media usage. When you post on your personal or professional page, you must ask yourself, "If this lands on the front page of the newspaper, would I be okay with it?"

Many educators do not treat their social media posts with that much care. They think that what they say and do on their own time is their own business. But this is an incredibly immature and naive way to perceive your sphere of influence. It is dangerous to imagine your social media posts will not have a direct impact on the respect people have for you.

Scroll through your social media pages. Pretend you are a prospective parent. Look at yourself from their lens. Are you proud of what you see? Or does it make you cringe? Deleting what is already out there probably will not help the cause, but being mindful from here on out is necessary. Make that commitment and you will not be sorry.

DEALING WITH PUBLICITY GONE WRONG

It's not just social media that impacts the way that people see you and the district. It's not just your emails and texts that influence others' perception. As a high leader, it seems that your very existence is constantly telling a story.

Professional titles follow leaders everywhere. Everywhere. At the grocery store, people will recognize you as the assistant principal. At the neighborhood barbecue, someone will suddenly come up to you and greet you as the principal. On the front row at the concert, someone will recognize you. "Aren't you the Chief Business Official?"

Or, horror of horrors, you will humbly attend the school conference for your fiancée's daughter, only be recognized as an Assistant Superintendent. Suddenly, you're being called out. How dare the Assistant Superintendent attend a parent teacher conference?

You were asked by your fiance to attend his daughter's first grade parent teacher conference to discuss her reading struggles. You didn't attend as an administrator, but as a caring and loving soon-to-be stepmom. You're genuinely concerned about your daughter's reading, and you want to hear more information about how to better help her. But suddenly you're being accused of having a conflict of interest.

You sit in the meeting intently listening, because you want to use your background as a reading specialist to ultimately help your future step-daughter. You're there as a support to your fiancé's daughter. Your intentions are rock-solid, and the school administration thanks you for being there.

But you soon realize you can't even attend parent teacher conferences without causing drama and rocking your world. Before long, you've been accused by her mother of misusing your professional status. Your character is called into question. Emails are sent to your superintendent. Complaints are expressed to the board (in public open session). The mom states that you were hurting this student's academic progress with your attendance.

To say that you feel humiliation is an understatement. Fair? No. Irrational Complaint? Yes. And yet the lesson you learned here is invaluable: Once an administrator, always an administrator. Once a principal, always a principal. Once a superintendent, always a superintendent. You fill in the title.

It's easy to see that leaders live in a cruel, judgmental world. However, if you have an "I don't give a crap what people think of me attitude," you will not last in the world of school leadership. Even when your intentions are pure, you're just having a jolly good time, and it seems your actions aren't impacting anyone else, it is absolutely critical to pause often and look at yourself from the outside.

Put yourself in check. Remember, you are *serving* families. Families of conservatives, democrats, and families which are highly passionate about a range of issues. Your job is not to position yourself to fit the mold of any one of them. Your job is to be approachable by *all* of them. As soon as your families and staff form a perception that you are now unapproachable, you should probably start looking for your next job.

Prevention here is key. Be careful about what you do, what you post, and how you are perceived. An ounce of prevention is worth a pound of cure.

THE TRUE NORTH

Branding is exhausting. It can sometimes feel a little like you are the mayor. The reality is that you are a public official. You are responsible for the future of the youth of your community. You are ensuring that your community's families *trust* you with their cargo.

It's important to send out a consistent, responsible, and professional message to the people in your care. Build their confidence and mold their thoughts in a positive way. Your district will thank you.

NOTES

1. Tobias Van Schneider, "If You Want It, You Might Get It. The Reticular Activating System Explained," Accessed November 9, 2021, https://medium.com/desk-of-van-schneider/if-you-want-it-you-might-get-it-the-reticular-activating-system-explained-761b6ac14e53.

2. "Visual Standards: A Guide to Wichita Public Schools Visual Communication Standards," Accessed November 9, 2021, https://www.usd259.org/Page/14880.

3. "Superintendent's Strategic Plan Van—Graduation+ and the Future Ready Center at North High," Accessed November 9, 2021, Video: 10:01, https://www.youtube.com/watch?v=l73Mf5JH2S0&ab_channel=WichitaPublicSchools.

4. Wichita Public Schools YouTube Channel https://www.youtube.com/channel/UCwhhaQp1bOE4NpAD2BKjlQw.

5. "10 Districts with Awesome Brands," *Advancing K12*, Accessed November 9, 2021, https://www.skyward.com/discover/blog/skyward-blogs/skyward-executive-blog/october-2018/10-districts-with-awesome-brands.

6. Ibid.

7. Ibid.

8. "Brand Identity Toolkit," Wichita Public Schools, Accessed November 9, 2021, https://www.usd259.org/Page/15241.

9. "The Power of Branding: Telling Your School's Story," Accessed November 9, 2021, http://www.jsanfelippo.com/appearances/.

10. Simon Sinek, *Start with Why.*

Chapter 10

The Journey

Remembering the End Goal

This book began by reflecting on a quote by William Arthur Ward: "The pessimist complains about the wind; the optimist expects it to change; the realist adjusts the sails."

The journey of administration is a difficult one, fraught with difficulty, pain, and lack of popularity. Optimism often dies early in the journey. It's easy to begin complaining, resenting your position, and wishing you were somewhere else.

How can you change your focus? How can you stay away from complaining, while also steering clear of unrealistic optimism? How can you learn to enjoy the journey, simply adjusting the sails?

DEVELOPING RESILIENCE

To survive the journey, you will need endless amounts of resilience. As a leader, you are faced with countless unexpected situations. You deal with one curve ball after another. As soon as you become comfortable with one set of guidelines or policies, state or federal initiatives come down the pipe to change everything once again.

Your superiors don't seem to recognize the stress this causes. They expect you to embrace the new policies with open arms, saying, "Yay! Let's adjust yet again!" The constant changes wear you down. You run on adrenaline, never truly having the time to rest. You end many days wondering what new administrative "fire" you will have to put out tomorrow.

In the process, it's easy to fall into unrealistic optimism or unproductive pessimism. Your goal should be to focus on uncompromising resilience.

Unrealistic Optimism

You can hope all you want. You can put on a good face and think positively. You can live optimistically and hope for the best. But ultimately, empty enthusiasm doesn't go far when faced with the unrelenting challenges of top leadership.

Practically, hope will not solve your challenges. You can tell your students, "I hope you pass your AP exam," but your good desires don't ultimately change the outcome of their tests. Muttering to yourself, "I hope that irate parent will leave me alone" will certainly not deescalate the situation. Your hopes do not ultimately change the relationship with the parent. Hope is a desire for a certain thing to happen, and hope by itself is powerless.

Instead of aimlessly hoping, you must be ready to take action. You must prepare for battle by showing up each and every day, ready to face the challenges of your position. You must be ready to hear the angry parent out, listening with intention even when the going gets tough.

Hopeful thinking doesn't change things, but action does. You can face that parent squarely. You can feel like a badass as she leaves your office, knowing that even though she did not get her way, she respects your calm demeanor, logical behavior, and honesty.

Unproductive Pessimism

On the other side of the spectrum, it's easy to fall into hopeless pessimism. Realizing how hard your position is, you give in to self-pity and sadness. Losing all hope and optimism, you complain about the discomforts of your job.

To complain is to express dissatisfaction or annoyance with something. The leader that constantly complains without action is flat-out irritating. It is easy to fall into this trap, but you need to realize that complaining is a one-way street to nowhere.

As a leader, you are being bombarded with 101 problems every day. Isn't it okay to let off a little steam? Sure, it can be a healthy thing to vent to your work colleagues or best friend about a crappy situation. But please caution yourself against being one of those ramblers. As a productive leader, you don't want to be one of those people who goes on and on about problems.

So do your venting quickly. Do it and be done with it. Fast. You have the problem to solve, so get to work on that.

Uncompromising Resilience

The goal is to be a realist. You want to be a person who accepts a situation as it is and is prepared to deal with it accordingly. But that's hard to do when reality seems to change every few days, at seemingly random intervals.

Rather than just hoping for the best or complaining about the worst, you can learn to adjust. Adjusting means adapting to a new situation. When you learn to bounce back and adjust, you've found the sweet spot. Rather than being a victim to your problems, you become the driver of outcomes. A realist that may not like the change, but he or she learns to deal with it effectively and efficiently.

What does this even mean? How does a leader go about doing this? You may have heard the saying: "You cannot teach old dogs new tricks." For leaders, this is simply *not* true. You will find that with experience comes a beautiful maturity.

This resilience and realism doesn't happen automatically at the start of your career. Instead, it grows little by little through your joys, trials, and mistakes. It is through the heartache and leadership failures that you will grow into a confident, vulnerable, and approachable leader.

Your tolerance for change becomes increasingly greater. Adjusting becomes easier. You do not necessarily like the changes. You do not welcome the bureaucracy, the difficult Union negotiations, or the constant mandates being passed down to you. But at the same time, you recognize that this is, in fact, what you signed up for.

You are not given the option to opt out of conflict, change, difficult conversations, or the implementation of new guidelines. Instead, you must conquer these situations head on. Adaptation is the path of true reward. Can you imagine the feeling you will experience when you adapt and conquer, eventually bringing the situation to a resolution? It's an amazing feeling, which will have the power to catapult you to the next level in your career.

You recognize that this resilience can grow over time and with experience. But how can you accelerate the process of learning? How can you gain skills so you can roll with the punches? It can be hard to get back up and keep going, day after day, in response to unending changes. How can you build resilience more quickly so that these changes don't knock you down?

Seek out Affirming Friends

As a leader, you need a little affirmation from time to time. You need to hear someone telling you that you are indeed rock star status. Unfortunately, you won't hear it enough. Most of the time, you will be bombarded with negative reviews, critiques, and criticism. The message of all these words is the same: you should be doing something different. Something better.

"You did not return my phone call fast enough."
"You did not make sure my kid got on the right bus."
"When you suspended my troublemaker, why wasn't the kid who initiated the fight suspended too?"

The list goes on and on. Quite frankly, these words you keep hearing are outright attacks.

Remember, your job may be thankless. So you need to surround yourself with people who know your value and will remind you of your inherent worth. Find a support system. If your spouse, siblings, and parents do not provide this kind of encouragement, find a friend, church group, or peer support system. Perhaps there is a social media community who will provide much-needed support and camaraderie.

Networking with colleagues can be a powerful source of resilience. You'll gain valuable encouragement from other leaders who are running similar types of schools. With them, you'll be able to totally vent and be transparent.

You'll be able to share your struggles openly, in a way you can't do within your own organization or building. You'll be able to let off steam: "I have this student who says he's going to shoot up the school. And now I have parents who don't want their kids to come to this school. How do I get over this? What do I do?"

Your friends will remind you that it happens. The situations you face are a daunting task for anyone to overcome. But when you have high-quality friends, you'll no longer feel like you are bearing that burden alone. Being able to talk transparently, get advice, and talk through your problems is a huge step towards resolution.

The challenges of leadership are enormous, and it's hard to know how to overcome them. A big way is to find collaboration and affirmation through colleagues, in the same district or outside it.

AFFIRM YOURSELF

Second, you must pause and thank yourself. You are the one who truly knows the hard work you put in day after day. You must applaud and reward yourself for the effort you exert. And how is that done?

Self-care. Sure, you say it is important to take some time for yourself. Practically, what does that look like? And how can you even spare a few minutes to yourself, much less a weekend? How can you learn to balance home life and work life?

You may not know how, but you must do it. No exceptions. Some are lucky enough to have a strong support system of family or friends who are willing to lend a hand so they can take a break. Others are not so fortunate, and are going at this wild ride all alone.

So what if you are one of those that are doing this all alone? Use your work schedule to your advantage. As administrators, you have a bit more freedom. The work can get done when the work gets done. It does not have to happen between 7:30 am–4:30 p.m. You do not keep banker hours.

If that means you take a two-hour lunch to clear your mind from the morning chaos, take the long lunch! You have people at work who can make sure things are taken care of while you take care of yourself. Do not ever let leaders tell you that the amount of time you spend in your day job equals success. This is a myth! Exhaustion is not a status symbol. Play hard, but also take time to rest hard.

You know what it takes to get your job done and to get it done well. On some days, you will put in 16 hours and exercise maximum productivity. Other days, you will be flat-out tapped. Two hours will be your max. After that, you just lose productivity.

Do not beat yourself up for the two-hour days. Those restful days are absolutely critical to your success. Just as an athlete must have recovery days to drive peak performance, so do you. Make sure you prioritize working for a superintendent and leadership team who carries out this same philosophy. Otherwise, do not be surprised if you experience burnout early on in your administrative career.

Take time for prayer, meditation, or your preferred method of decompression. Invest in travel, fitness, or working out. You don't have to work out like a crazy person. But at least get your mind distracted by going on a walk and looking at the flowers and the birds.

Whatever your preferred stress-relief activity is, do it. It's easy to forget to take care of yourself. You're often focused on solutions. You only want to solve the problem. You run it over and over in your mind and dwell on it. You overthink and become anxious. You forget the other strategies available to you.

Self-care activities are actually a way of helping solve the problem. They put you in a mental space to be able to go back and tackle the problem. These activities are giving your brain a break.

Self-care gives you time to reflect. It helps you develop the difficult skill of waiting. As you discipline yourself to *not* continue working on the problem, your mind has time to recalibrate, rejuvenate, and come back to the problem from a new perspective.

For a strong leader, waiting is extremely difficult. It's an art that takes practice. When a tough problem comes your way, discipline yourself to step aside and care for yourself. Rather than reacting, give the situation some time.

Instead of rushing to make a rash decision, stop and wait. Think on it. Even though you desperately want to make this decision today, there is a true gift in being able to wait it out. You allow yourself to spend time processing, reflecting, and thinking through it.

You might decide to give the situation a day, or two, or three. If over the next few days, the issue still feels as urgent as it was on day one, then it's probably right to go with your gut. But often, during that waiting period of reflection, a new approach comes to your mind. Since you've taken the time to pray, go on a walk, and play a board game with your kids, your brain got a break. You can go back to the issue and figure out how to deal with it with a fresh perspective.

You will not be able to exercise resilience or bounce back from changes unless you have taken good care of yourself. So make sure you incorporate the rest you need into your daily and weekly schedule. Self-care is an important way to say thank you to yourself for the tireless work you put into the district.

PATIENT ENDURANCE

One of the most important ingredients of resilience is pure tenacity. Through experience, you must grow your ability to keep working through the really dark times of administration. When the parent complaints don't seem to go away, you must keep going. When the student behaviors are super extreme, you must never throw in the towel. When you have difficult staff members who are trying to make your life miserable, you must always move forward.

You must develop the grit to keep going through these common dark places in an administrator's professional life. The reality is that you'll get to the point you're ready to be done or look for another job. Resilience means you keep pressing forward, no matter what. As you develop this tenacity, it's critical to keep in mind the end goal.

REMEMBER THE END GOAL

When the job of leadership becomes almost more than you can bear, it's important to remember the legacy you are leaving. You can enjoy the journey because it is worth it. Use the following list to renew your vision and your energy. Your job is worthwhile, and it's making a difference.

You are a change-maker inspiring students to reach their full potential in preparation for life beyond the classroom. As you create a mission and value that helps students find their interests and focus on their goals, you transform the trajectory of their lives. In your role as administrator, you are truly impacting society. As one author summed it up, "Regardless of the impressive policies and procedures you implement, the kids in your schools are the legacy you leave behind."[1]

You are in the service industry. When you feel the weight of the world on your shoulders, the fact that you are serving others makes that weight bearable to carry. You are serving teachers, students, families, and an entire community. Though you may sometimes feel distanced from the actual task of learning in the classrooms, remember that without your tireless work, none of that would be possible.

The camaraderie with other teachers and administrators makes it worth it. You stand together with your colleagues, sharing war stories and together problem solving to overcome the battle each and every day. You are a valued member of a team. You have the privilege to lead a high-quality team with similar values, missions, and dreams. And the relationship is not a one-way street. The teachers and staff on your team give back by helping you learn and grow as well.

Legacy is about other people around you. Through the goals you set and the dreams you create, you impact others' futures. Through your effective branding, you share those dreams with the world. You must remember that "your leadership legacy— . . . the influence you have on the thoughts, actions and lives of the people you lead—is being built now. It already is reflected in the individual faces of each person you come in contact with at work."[2]

Your legacy is also about you as a person. You are leaving an impact that directly reflects your unique, one-of-a-kind perspective. No one can leave the exact impact that you can on your district and community. You must remember that "legacy thinking is about you—as an individual . . . with personal hopes, goals, desires and expectations. You want to do your best for the school district, but you also want to be at peace with yourself. Have you found satisfaction in your job? Are you doing the things you want to be doing? Are you playing to your innate strengths? Are you in your natural role? Or are you constantly pushing or pressuring yourself far outside of your comfort zone to achieve the organizational goals before you? Legacy thinking calls all of these questions into play."[3]

As you work within your natural gifting, you will experience a deep sense of satisfaction. You will begin to see the ways that our job as an administrator is making a long-term impact. To keep yourself focused on your end goal in the midst of turmoil, remember the ways that you as a unique individual have been called to impact the community.

What is your unique, personalized goal? Do you want to leave behind a legacy of high-quality strategic processes in your organization? Do you want to teach others communication skills? Will you enrich your teachers and principals with high-quality continuing education opportunities? Will you be remembered for your innovation, creativity, and futuristic thinking?[4] Each of these is a legitimate desire, a way that you can leave your fingerprint on the lives you touch.

Your investment in your school and district can make long-term difference in other people's lives. The choices you make and the direction you take can "impact future generations."[5] You can "do something that will last beyond [your] lifetime and that really matters."[6] You can make an impact that leaves a legacy for those who follow.[7] Remember, "your legacy is, quite simply, what people will do differently because they were part of your district leadership."[8] What legacy will you leave today?

THE TRUE NORTH

Being a classroom teacher is visibly rewarding and immediately gratifying. It's obvious that you are making a difference. But as an administrator, it's harder to see the rewards. It's easy to drown in the difficulties and forget the difference you are making.

To choose an administrative career means you embrace risk and stress. Your career requires guts, heartbreak, and extreme anxiety. Making a difference through administration is a whole different ballgame than teaching.

Whether you are a current school or district leader looking for a little extra affirmation or a new administrator ready to embark on your first job, know that your service to your community is absolutely needed. Although your job is often thankless, you know that you are making a difference every day in the lives of your students and your community.

If you can't see the rewards right now, take it by faith: your job is needed. The journey of school administration, with all its highs and lows, is well worth it.

No matter the challenges, you will succeed. You will have an amazing career. You will need to develop an incredible amount of resilience and courage. You'll pivot when you need to, and learn to bounce back from trials. But ultimately, you will come out victorious.

Pivot when you need to. Bounce back from trials. It's okay to change course when your gut and evidence are aligned. When the winds are strong, adjust the sails. Just remember: always keep heading to your ultimate destination. The end goal is worth it. And don't forget to enjoy the journey.

NOTES

1. "5 Reasons You Should Become a Superintendent," Last modified February 22, 2017, Accessed November 23, 2021, https://blog.cuw.edu/5-reasons-to-become-a-superintendent-2163/.

2. Robert Galford, "Legacy Planning: How Will You Be Remembered?" *AASA: The School Superintendents Association,* Accessed November 23, 2021, https://www.aasa.org/SchoolAdministratorArticle.aspx?id=6470.

3. Ibid.

4. Michael Chirichello, "Lasting Legacies," *Focus Magazine,* February 2018, Vol. 39, No. 1, Accessed November 23, 2021, https://learningforward.org/wp-content/uploads/2018/03/lasting-legacies.pdf.

5. Ibid.

6. Ibid.

7. Ibid.

8. Robert Galford, "Legacy Planning: How Will You Be Remembered?"

Bibliography

"10 Districts with Awesome Brands." *Advancing K12*. Accessed November 9, 2021. https://www.skyward.com/discover/blog/skyward-blogs/skyward-executive-blog/october-2018/10-districts-with-awesome-brands.

"21st Century Schools and the Role of the CBO." *Casbo 2014 Annual Conference*. Accessed December 2, 2021. https://dcgstrategies.com/wp-content/uploads/2015/07/Workshop-Supplement-CASBO-2014-21st-Century-Schools.pdf.

"5 Reasons You Should Become a Superintendent." Last modified February 22, 2017. https://blog.cuw.edu/5-reasons-to-become-a-superintendent-2163/.

"Brand Identity Toolkit." Wichita Public Schools. Accessed November 9, 2021. https://www.usd259.org/Page/15241.

Brown, Brené. *Daring Greatly.* New York City: Avery, 2015.

Chirichello, Michael. "Lasting Legacies." *Focus Magazine,* February 2018, Vol. 39, No. 1. https://learningforward.org/wp-content/uploads/2018/03/lasting-legacies.pdf.

"Every Student Future Ready: The WPS Strategic Plan 2018–2023." Accessed November 9, 2021. https://www.usd259.org/cms/lib/KS01906405/Centricity/Domain/4393/StratPlan-Year4-Spreads.pdf.

Feltman, Charles. *The Thin Book of Trust: An Essential Primer for Building Trust at Work.* Bend, OR: Thin Book Publishing, 2021. In "Highlights of The Thin Book of Trust: An Essential Primer for Building Trust at Work," https://www.tacoma.uw.edu/sites/default/files/2020-09/thinbookoftrust.pdf.

Galford, Robert. "Legacy Planning: How Will You Be Remembered?" *AASA: The School Superintendents Association.* Accessed November 23, 2021. https://www.aasa.org/SchoolAdministratorArticle.aspx?id=6470.

Kuktelionis, Casey. "The Four Most Important Questions to Ask when Rounding." Last modified on January 15, 2021. https://www.studereducation.com/important-questions-ask-rounding/.

Maxwell, John. *Failing Forward: How to Make the Most of Your Mistakes.* Nashville: Thomas Nelson, 2007.

Maxwell, John. *Leadership Gold: Lessons I've Learned from a Lifetime of Leading.* New York: HarperCollins Leadership, 2008.

Miller, Jo. "The Secret to a Good Meeting: The Meeting before the Meeting," Last modified on July 23, 2018. https://www.theladders.com/career-advice/the-secret-to-a-good-meeting-the-meeting-before-the-meeting.

"Nonviolent Communication - M. Rosenberg (summary)." Last modified December 1, 2015. https://www.mudamasters.com/en/personal-growth-effectiveness/nonviolent-communication-mrosenberg-summary.

"QAPI Leadership Rounding Guide." Accessed November 9, 2021. https://www.cms.gov/medicare/provider-enrollment-and-certification/qapi/downloads/qapileadershiproundingtool.pdf.

Reina, Michelle. "How Leaders Build Trust, One Mistake at a Time." *Reina Trust Building.* Accessed November 29, 2021. https://reinatrustbuilding.com/how-leaders-build-trust-one-mistake-at-a-time/.

Roosevelt, Theodore. In Erin McCarthy, "Roosevelt's 'The Man in the Arena,'" *Mental Floss,* Last modified April 23, 2020, Accessed December 2, 2021, https://www.mentalfloss.com/article/63389/roosevelts-man-arena.

Scott, Susan. *Fierce Conversations: Achieving Success at Work and in Life One Conversation At A Time.* New York City: Berkley, 2004.

Siddiqui, Mehreen and Alexis Lennahan. "Corner Office Chats: The Importance of Learning Public Speaking Skills." Goal Set Coach, December 17, 2020. YouTube video. 20:22 https://www.youtube.com/watch?v=Cp7yoiMV4_s&ab_channel=GoalSetCoach.

Sinek, Simon. *Start with Why: How Great Leaders Inspire Everyone to Take Action.* New York City: Portfolio, 2011. In Sam T. Davis, "Start with Why by Simon Sinek," Accessed December 2, 2021, https://www.samuelthomasdavies.com/book-summaries/business/start-with-why/.

"Summary of Difficult Conversations: How to Discuss What Matters Most." Accessed November 22, 2021. https://www.beyondintractability.org/bksum/stone-difficult.

"Superintendent Dr. Alicia Thompson Shares Feedback from Listening Sessions." Wichita Public Schools. Accessed November 17, 2021. https://www.usd259.org/site/default.aspx?PageType=3&DomainID=2766&ModuleInstanceID=13639&ViewID=6446EE88-D30C-497E-9316-3F8874B3E108&RenderLoc=0&FlexDataID=22054&PageID=8977.

"Superintendent's Strategic Plan Van—Graduation+ and the Future Ready Center at North High." Accessed November 9, 2021. Video: 10:01. https://www.youtube.com/watch?v=l73Mf5JH2S0&ab_channel=WichitaPublicSchools.

The Academies Charter Management Organization 2019–2024 Strategic Plan.

"The Power of Branding: Telling Your School's Story." Accessed November 9, 2021. http://www.jsanfelippo.com/appearances/.

"The Six Minute Book Summary of the Book, Fierce Conversations, by Susan Scott." Last modified on August 23, 2011. Accessed November 29, 2021. http://rustedpumpkin.com/rugh-blog/the-six-minute-book-summary-of-the-book-fierce-conversations-by-susan-scot.

Van Schneider, Tobias. "If You Want It, You Might Get It. The Reticular Activating System Explained." Accessed November 9, 2021. https://medium.com/

desk-of-van-schneider/if-you-want-it-you-might-get-it-the-reticular-activating-system-explained-761b6ac14e53.

"Visual Standards: A Guide to Wichita Public Schools Visual Communication Standards." https://www.usd259.org/Page/14880.

Voss, Chris. *Never Split the Difference.* New York City: Harper Business, 2016.

Wichita Public Schools Channel. https://www.youtube.com/channel/UCwhhaQp1bOE4NpAD2BKjlQw.

Willink, Jocko, and Babin, Leif. *Extreme Ownership: How U.S. Navy Seals Lead and Win.* New York: St. Martin's Press, 2017.

About the Author

Donya Ball, EdD, is a district superintendent in California. She is a change maker in public education, leading staff to inspire students to reach their full potential in preparation for life beyond the classroom. She has worked in education for over 20 years serving in various administrative capacities at both the site and district level. She presents at local and national conferences and works as adjunct faculty teaching aspiring administrators.

Made in the USA
Columbia, SC
14 May 2023

16511839R00079